1-800-

WHAT MUST I DO?

MAKE YOUR JUICER YOUR DRUG STORE

Dr. Laura Newman

Foreword by John B. Lust

Benedict Lust Publications, New York, N.Y. 10156

WHAT MUST I DO?
Make Your Juicer Your Drug Store
Beneficial Books are Published by
BENEDICT LUST PUBLICATIONS
NEW YORK, NEW YORK 10156-0404 U.S.A

This Beneficial Book edition includes every word contained in Laura Newman's original higher-priced edition entitled, Make Your Garden Your Drug Store, plus a new forward by John B. Lust, N.D. It is printed from new plates made from completely reset, clear, easy-to-read type.

PRINTING HISTORY
Continuously published since the first
Beneficial Book edition / January 1970
All Rights Reserved
This book may not be reproduced in whole or in part by any means without written permission from the publisher.
Copyright © 1970 by Benedict Lust Publications
Copyright © 1992 by Benedict Lust Publications

Publisher's Note: *Where any condition has progressed to a serious stage, or if uncertainty exists as to the seriousness, it is best not to delay timely professional services of a competent physician.*

ISBN 0-87904-001-7

Library of Congress Catalog Number 76-125414

Printed in the United States Of America

FOREWORD

Only nature can perform the complete life process—the transformation of inorganic substances from out of the earth into organic plants to be consumed by animals and human beings. This is nature's LIFE LINE.

Unfortunately for us, "modernism" and "civilization," with a powerful assist from the hucksters on Madison Avenue, have contributed to the development of today's average man. A man whose vital chemistry is denatured, deficient and unbalanced, unable to enjoy his life as it goes by.

To revitalize the chemistry of your body, you must consume vitally perfect food. Cooking and chemical interference change the natural properties of food. The use of heat above body temperature destroys food values. Those processes should be avoided. But how?

LIFE SUSTAINS LIFE is a principal law of nature. You can find within the framework of this law the ideal method to obtain a rich natural source of vitamins, minerals, enzymes, proteins and amino acids—building blocks for your body to be consistently well, disease resistant and beautiful—presented to you in the pages of this book. Fresh raw fruit and vegetable juices, nature's own LIFE LINE!

When we consider that vegetables and fruits have been naturally cooked by solar energy; that they contain all the elements the sun and earth have buried deep into their fibre cells; that they are live-cell foods —is it not logical to assume if we extract the juices from the cells of these fresh fruits and vegetables, and put their health-giving fluid into our blood, we will receive its vital energy? Thanks to the invention of electric vegetable juicers we are able to take the coarsest vegetable, put it in the hopper of the machine and press out almost instantly the juice of the plant, with all of its life and energy, no matter how tough and dry the vegetable may seem.

I hope the hundreds of thousands who have read my books, *Raw Juice Therapy* and *Drink Your Troubles Away*, will be as happy as I was to discover this informative book. In it Laura Newman, through study and practice, compiled a wealth of knowledge for more than 13 years. She has detailed a tremendous amount of useful advice. Through it your juicer will not only become a source of healthful nourishment, but it will become more valuable to you than a gold mine. I express my heartfelt thanks to her for what she has so freely given me to pass on to you.

John B. Lust
Beaumont, California
June 1, 1970

PREFACE TO THE FOURTH EDITION

My earnest wish has always been that the books I write and publish would reach you and millions like you. These unique books based on a simple natural philosophy, are reliable guides for your practical application of "natural living" principles.

Now, with the fourth mass printing of *Make Your Juicer Your Drug Store*, I'm truly grateful that my wish has been granted.

I thank God for this blessing.

Westlake Village, Calif.
July, 1978

John B. Lust, Publisher

TABLE OF CONTENTS

Page

INTRODUCTION

WHAT MUST I DO?

This is a question people are asking themselves today. In almost every home you find sickness and suffering, and most people haven't the faintest idea that they, themselves, are causing their own misery.

Only by an application of the knowledge of food and its properties can we keep the body in perfect health. Knowledge, and the will to use that knowledge, are the weapons against Disease. Nature does not excuse the careless, and ignorance is rewarded with disaster.

You can make yourself well or ill according to the food you consume, and millions of people are unconsciously committing suicide daily at their own tables.

Before a person can hope to select his diet intelligently, he must first learn something about the value of his food and what minerals and vitamins it contains.

The way to salvation from pain and suffering can only be reached by the efforts of the sufferer himself. However, Nature can work miracles if one only co-operates with her intelligently and gives her the materials to work with. Instead of reaching for the bottle off the drug store shelf and thus suppressing disease, make your juicer your drug store and eat and drink your way to health. In this way you cleanse the system of its toxic poisons and build up new health, beauty and youthfulness in Nature's way.

The theory of body building through nutritional elements is not to be interpreted as entering the field of medicine or as violating a doctor's prerogative. Our purpose is simply to improve vitality through proper nutrition.

If any dangerous acute conditions exist or are suspected, we strongly advise consulting a diet-conscious physician.

In the words of Dr. Jonathan Foreman: "The basic training and creed of the Medical Profession is based upon the healing and caring of the sick. It is not within their province nor is it their responsibility to keep people from getting sick. THAT IS THEIR OWN INDIVIDUAL RESPONSIBILITY. The medical profession therefore works on effects rather than causes."

Charles Noyes Kinney, Emeritus Professor of Chemistry, Drake University, Des Moines, Iowa, in his book, "Nutrition", differentiating between Foods and Medicine or Drugs, states: "A food is a substance which when taken into the system furnishes required elements which enter into and become a part of cell structure, or which aids in building up and maintaining cell life and activity. It must also provide elements required to carry out the by-products of cell building and waste products, and all the many vital life processes involved. A drug or medicine may stimulate or modify cell activity, but it furnishes no material for maintenance. The crack of a whip or the electric current may stimulate, but they do nothing to maintain or continue the action. Medicine therefore may modify some action, but it applies no material to sustain it."

The theory behind the value of raw vegetable juices is simply that they furnish the body with necessaay materials for body functioning and repair—materials which are so often missing from the average diet. In this way, Nature is given an abundance of proper materials in an easily assimilable form, and is thus assisted in her efforts to return the body to normal functioning.

If you were raising animals, you would realize how important proper diet is, and you would put that knowledge into effect. While the diets suggested herewith have been selected with the utmost care, and while hundreds of letters have been received telling of the seemingly miraculous results attained through raw vegetable juices, we wish to make it clearly understood that these diets are merely suggestive and no claim is made by us as to the curative properties of any particular juice or combination of juices.

CHAPTER 1

MAN DOES NOT DIE—HE KILLS HIMSELF

This is what the wise Seneca stated long ago in early Rome. Science is just now beginning to prove that this is true. Everywhere people are committing involuntary suicide at their own tables with their knives and forks, dying from disease wrought by improper diet.

People formerly thought that disease was the work of the devils and of the spirits of the wicked dead. Folks afflicted with a disease were believed to be "possessed with devils," and medicine men or witch doctors of those days poured vile concoctions down the throats of their patients to drive out these evil spirits.

Most people still have only a hazy idea as to what constitutes a disease. They believe it to be something mysterious that "attacks" them and consider there is very little that they, personally, can do about it. There is no real understanding of the functioning of their body or how it depends for its strength and health upon the food consumed.

Some people even go so far as to consider sickness and disease a cross given them to bear by the Lord, not realizing what a wonderful body they possess and that there is everything in Nature to keep that body in perfect health. It is their own lack of knowledge or failure to use that knowledge that has brought about their regrettable condition.

10

Dr. George D. Crile, who was head of the Crile Clinic in Cleveland, and one of the world's greatest surgeons, said, "There is no NATURAL death. All deaths from so-called natural causes are merely the end-point of a progressive acid saturation."

Sir William Arbuthnot Lane, a world authority on medical matters and long regarded as England's foremost abdominal surgeon, said, "There is but one disease—deficient drainage."

He also said at another time, when entertained by the staff of Johns Hopkins Hospital and Medical College: "Gentlemen, I will never die of cancer. I am taking measures to prevent it . . . It is caused by poisons created in our bodies by the food we eat . . . What we should do, then, if we would avoid cancer, is to eat whole wheat bread and raw fruit and vegetables; first, that we may be better nourished; second, that we may more easily eliminate waste products . . . We have been studying germs when we should have been studying diet and drainage . . . The world has been on the wrong track. The answer has been within ourselves all the time. Drain the body of its poisons, feed it properly, and the miracle is done. Nobody need have cancer who will take the trouble to avoid it."

And what he said about cancer may well be applied to any disease.

And so, we find the cause of disease is chiefly two-fold:

1. Weakened cells.

2. Waste deposits in those weakened cells (deficient drainage.)

Surely it follows readily that the correction of ill health lies in assisting Nature to cleanse those waste poisons from the body and, through proper diet, to build up the cells so that the various organs can do their work properly.

Let us consider the cells of the body. These cells wear out and new cells take their place. This goes on every second of the day and night as long as we live, and the new cells can be no better than the material of which they are made. If we take plenty of natural foods containing the necessary minerals, vitamins and enzymes daily into our systems our cells should be strong, and should function properly, but if there is a deficiency of these elements, they will be weak, and degeneration will set in.

All of these essential elements are contained in the raw plants, if grown on proper soil, but man's diet consists chiefly of cooked foods—something he doesn't have to spend much time chewing. The cooking (especially when the food is boiled) destroys to a large extent the mineral and vitamin content and so a deficiency occurs in the body. It has thus been said that when Man first learned to cook his food disease was born.

You might ask, "From where does the waste matter come?" It comes from the vast amounts of demineralized, devitalized, dead foods which are daily dumped into the stomach of almost every individual. After that food is digested and absorbed into the blood stream, it is carried to all the cells and tissues of the body. The body eliminates what it can and the remainder settles in the weakest cells—those which are not strong enough to "clean house".

In this accumulating deposit of dead matter, germs, like scavengers, breed—rotting takes place and pus, mucous and other poisonous substances form. This we call "Disease", and the name of the particular disease depends upon the location of those poisons.

Thus it will be seen that there is, after all, only ONE DISEASE—deficient drainage! The name of the disease depends upon where these poisons settle; thus we have rheumatism, neuritis, sciatica, kidney trouble, liver trouble, gall bladder trouble or a thousand and one other "troubles", according to where this waste accumulation is deposited. And, remember, the poisons always settle where the cells are the weakest—where they are unable to discard what they do not need. The cells are weak because the diet has been deficient in the materials to keep them rebuilt properly.

Hence it will readily be seen how important it is to make sure that every day, the body receives all the materials to build healthy cells, and also to assist Nature in ridding the body of its accumulation of waste.

CHAPTER 2

WHAT SHALL I EAT OR DRINK?

According to some of the greatest scientists, practically every diseased condition is a result of a deficiency in the diet.

The teeth will decay if the diet is deficient in calcium, for calcium is needed in building the cells of teeth and bones. We can see what is happening to the teeth, but we cannot see what is happening to the bones.

A man needs in his food merely a trace of iodine—a tiny mite which we almost need a microscope to see, yet if he does not get it, he will sooner or later develop a goiter. Professor Max Schlapp, of the New York Post-Graduate Hospital, stated, "A lack of iodine in the diet of a pregnant mother may cause underdevelopment of the thyroid gland and brain of the embryo, resulting in an idiot. On the other hand, an abundance of iodine will lead to the birth of a child with a superior brain. Thus a minute quantity of iodine may determine whether the child will be an idiot or a genius. It is, therefore, important that a pregnant mother consume an abundance of organic iodine."

And note, he said "organic" iodine—the kind of iodine we find in plants.

The amount of iron in the entire body is only the merest trifle, but if we fail to obtain that amount we develop anemia.

Dr. Percy R. Howe, of Boston University, a man who has done most fundamental work in nutrition on monkeys, says that for every known deficiency in the feeding of monkeys, he can predict with absolute certainty what deficiency (disease) will show up. He also says that where it sometimes takes many weeks for these deficiencies to show after beginning the deficient feeding, yet this deficiency condition can be cleared up completely in a very few days after the food deficiency is restored to the diet.

Here the law of Nature works so distinctly that he can recognize the deficiency as always of the same character from withholding the same necessary chemicals.

Again we find an interesting illustration of the consequence of mineral deficiencies proved by another famous nutritional scientist. Dr. Elmer J. McCallum of Johns Hopkins University, Baltimore, took sixteen different groups of small animals and allowed each group to represent a body chemical, each group a different chemical, and by withholding from the first group calcium, the second group iron, the third potassium, the fourth sodium and so on through the entire sixteen groups, he could predict with certainty the sort of disease which would develop in each group. Every one of the minerals are required if Nature is to build strong, healthy cells so the body can function properly and, if weakness occurs, it is usually because there has not been a sufficient amount of the necessary materials.

Everyone, therefore, should have a working knowledge of foods and the proper care of the body.

"What shall I eat and drink?" is not the query of the crank or faddist, but the thoughtful question of the scientist, of the biologist, and of all those who are earnestly seeking health.

The first thing to ask, if you become ill, is, "Have I been eating something which is causing this distress, or is there a deficiency of a certain mineral or vitamin in my diet?"

And remember, all the minerals and vitamins are found in Nature—in fruits and vegetables, nuts, whole grains and sunshine.

It is not through a lack of quantity of food only that a deficiency occurs. It has been said that one-third of what we eat keeps us alive and the other two-thirds keeps the doctor alive, but the "food" eaten by most people is "dead" food and so the body dies. Most people are literally starving to death on a full stomach. So many grossly overeat of refined foods. It is a law of Nature that anything unused in the system is in the way and must be eliminated in order to restore harmony.

Every acute disease is merely a healing crisis—a result of the body struggling to free itself from its load of toxic poisons within. Every pimple or boil is the evidence of the body throwing off these poisons through the skin. A fever is the body's method of burning up the wastes. Nature does her best to keep the body clean and healthy, but we must co-operate.

CHAPTER 3

HOW OLD IS OLD?

To a school girl, 30 seems old. As she grows older she probably thinks of "old" as 50 or 60 years of age. And most people of 50 feel they are definitely on the skids. Perhaps they have felt that way long before they reached 50. They feel they will henceforth have to live a little more carefully. They expect to be stiff in the joints when they arise in the morning. They expect to have lowered resistance to colds, flu and other infectious diseases. They expect to be able to do less work. They expect to enjoy life less. They expect all this without trying to analyse "WHY?" and their expectations are fulfilled.

What a tragedy! What a useless waste of precious years of life! Everywhere one finds sickness and disease and comparatively few people living to even 80 years of age.

Now contrast this with a condition found by Dr. Robert McCarrison, who spent nine years as a doctor in a colony in the Himalayan region in Northern India. Here he found a remarkable race of people. At least it seems remarkable to us who are so used to early aging that we find his report almost incredible. In this region, it was a very common thing to find people over the century mark—in fact, some of these "Old Men" were recently married and raising families of healthy

children. When they were working in the fields
with the younger men, Dr. Robert McCarrison said
he could not tell the difference between the younger men and the older.

In the nine years that Dr. McCarrison spent in
this country he reports that there was absolutely
no sickness of any kind among these people and
that he would have been quite idle had it not been
for the sickness and surgery of the people at the
post, who lived on the usual "civilized" British
diet.

Why were these people so healthy and virile?
Look at what they ate and you will discover the
answer.

Their diet consisted of grains in their natural
state, nuts, vegetables and fruits, and most of this
was eaten raw. No animal food of any kind was
eaten except a little milk or cheese.

Dr. Robert McCarrison also performed a very
interesting and important laboratory experiment.
He selected a diet, similar to these people's, consisting of whole wheat flour, unleavened bread,
lightly smeared with butter, sprouted Bengal gram
(a legume), large quantities of fresh raw carrots and
cabbage and raw whole milk. To this he added a
small amount of raw meat and bones once a week.

He fed this diet to more than a thousand rats
and, although he kept them till they had reached
the equivalent of 50 to 60 human years, no rat
became ill.

Two thousand other rats, living in the same quarters, were fed diets of Indian people who are not so healthy. Those rats developed thirty-nine different diseases. These diseases were similar to human diseases and included two cases of cancer.

Old age is not a matter of years; it is a matter of how strong the cells of the body are, and that depends upon the materials of which they are made.

How many old people have you seen—old, stiff, crippled people in their twenties and thirties? And occasionally, even here, you see healthy, young people in their sixties and seventies. It's about time one stopped to wonder "WHY!"

Dr. Victor G. Heiser of the Rockefeller Foundation, in an address to the American Association for the Advancement of Science, predicted the production, by some scientifically-minded nation, of a superior race of men who will be leaders of the world. "It will be done," he said, "by scientific use of food. The prize will go to the nation which develops the food sense of its individuals. The first step is to stamp out the diseases which largely attack men from within. How to start this has been discovered only in the present generation in tissue changes which come from choice of food."

Dr. Brown, in speaking in Malvern Collegiate, Toronto, Canada, stated, "A race of larger stature, greater vigor, increased longevity and higher degree of cultural attainment is the reward to the nation that uses scientific discoveries in nutrition intelligently."

One great doctor has made this statement: "If disease could be eliminated it is quite possible that we might have another era of Methuselahs."

The mothers, cooks and chefs must become student dietitians and learn food so they can select intelligently. Many women are literally killing their families with kindness—cooking foods which please their perverted appetites, not realizing the untold misery she is inflicting upon them; not realizing that their meals are the cause of, for example, her husband's rheumatism, her child's anemia or enlarged tonsils, or her own constipation.

The "best" cook may be very easily the "worst" cook as far as the health of the family is concerned. The closer the diet consists of raw foods in their natural state, the closer does the diet approach perfection.

Each cook should study foods for the mineral and vitamin content, for only in that way can she be assured that her family is receiving everything it needs to keep the body young and strong and free from disease.

Dr. Flora Rose, retired dean of the Cornell University home economics department, stated, "You can live to be 150 years old if you eat right."
"The 150 years life span can all be enjoyed with vigorous health, too," she said, "if the proper diet is followed."

Her dietary chart to longevity and good health includes consumption of a pint of milk daily; two vegetables—one green and the other yellow and raw; two fruits, one a citrus; and whole grain products. Vitamin concentrates are recommended for persons who lead sedentary lives.

Vegetable juices are our best vitamin concentrates, for Nature has combined the vitamins in a form we never obtain artificially, and the natural foods contain vitamins which are not yet discovered.

"The best source of vitamins is the garden and market—not the drug store," Dr. Elmer V. McCollum of Johns Hopkins University, told Boston University students. "There are abundant resources for the maintenance of a high standard of nutrition without recourse to the drug store or laboratory for synthetic vitamins."

Almost every week there appears in the daily newspaper accounts of people who are living to almost incredible ages, or so it seems to us with our perverted idea of aging. Recently there appeared in a local paper this news item: "London, Oct. 10 (AP)—Moscow Radio reported today that Mahmet Busakov, a collective farmer in the mountain village of Kirakura, in Azerbaijan, has just reached the age of 140. The report said he has 112 children, grandchildren, great-grandchildren, and great-great-grandchildren. His wife is 117 and his oldest daughter 100."

Durling, the columnist, reports about the same time, of Georges Isaac Hughes of New Born, N.C., who became a proud father at the age of ninety-six.

From the University of California comes the news of experiments carried on by Prof. Agnes Fay Morgan, nutritional expert, and Helen Davidson Simms, research associate, with a filtrate factor of Vitamin B2, in connection with early aging. Animals fed on a diet, deprived of this mysterious vitamin, showed aging of the adrenal glands and other vital organs. Rats fed on this diet for several months appeared to age rapidly, showing subnormal growth and greying hair. Two Boston bull pups showed greying hair about the mouth. A black guinea pig turned grey. When large quantities of this missing vitamin was given, the deterioration was remedied very quickly; glandular and skin damage disappeared and greyed hair was restored to its natural color. The vitamin is present in yeast, liver, rice, milk, and many vegetables, but when these are cooked the vitamin is lost. It is hard to get enough of these foods into the system except in the form of raw juice, so the quickest way to correct the resultant trouble is through the copious intake of juice from the vegetables containing this factor. This is chiefly the green, leafy vegetables, and especially the green alfalfa.

In the magazine section of the Rocky Mountain News, appeared an interesting article by Ernest La France and Sid Ross. This article was entitled, "Can We Live to be 120?", and brought out some striking highlights in the search for longevity by some of the world's scientists. Dr. Thomas S. Gardner, of Rutherford, N. J., and his associate, Edward Wenis, after years of research on thousands of guinea pigs, mice, and fruit flies, have reached the conclusion that victory over age is within our grasp, and made this startling statement: "In ten years, with the proper research, we could probably double the life span so the average person could live to be about 120 years!" They added that man would also enjoy good health to the very end.

Dr. Gardner and Edward Wenis have already kept a guinea pig in excellent health to the equivalent of 148 human years through a high vitamin diet and nucleic acid. Other outstanding findings in this field are:

1. Dr. Henry Clegg Sherman, professor-emeritus at Columbia's department of chemistry, has increased the life span of rats by 10% by increasing intake of Vitamin A alone.

2. Australian scientist, Dr. T. B. Robertson, has increased the life span of mice by 17% by feeding them nucleic acid, a component of yeast.

3. Dr. Anton J. Carlson of the University of Chicago added 20% to the life span of rats simply by having them fast one day in three or four.

4. Dr. C. M. McCay of Cornell increased the life span of rats over 50% by restricting caloric intake and adding minerals and vitamins.

There is no set number of years at which we can say we are old. "Old" is simply a degeneration of the body brought about by wrong feeding and living habits. Remember, no matter how many years you have lived, there is no cell in the body more than seven years old and, if you will eat, drink, and think properly, you will have a young, virile body. However, no one can do it for you—it's up to you.

CHAPTER 4

MALNUTRITION UNIVERSAL

The majority of people do not realize just how common it is to find deficiencies of minerals and vitamins in the diet, but the situation is none the less very serious. Most people drag along not knowing that they could just as well be strong and well and enjoying every minute of their trip through life.

"Only one person in a thousand escapes malnutrition." That is the conclusion of a survey published by the Ellen H. Richards Institute at Pennsylvania State College.

The survey took six years and is one of the most thorough ever made. It included both adults and children. The report is made in the college's chemistry leaflet, by Dr. Pauline Beery Mack, director of the Institute, and her associates.

Sixty per cent of the growing children were more than six months retarded in skeletal growth. The bones of a large majority of both adults and children were not satisfactorily mineralized.

In one city where the depression had been acute, one child out of every three examined gave evidence of having had rickets, the malnutrition bone trouble, due to lack of calcium and Vitamin D.

More than half of the people examined had iron and protein deficiencies which resulted in anemia.

Most of the people in the study group were not aware of any actual illness due to food deficiencies, but the border line deficiencies build up to major disorders in later years.

This condition was alarmingly illustrated by Canadian statistics. Out of 50,000 young men who tried to enlist in the active service army during one three month's period, 20,000 or 40% were rejected as medically unfit. Such a prevalence of ill health and malnutrition in the youth of a country which has enormous productive resources and a huge annual exportable surplus of food-stuffs, argues terrible mismanagement of national affairs.

A government investigation disclosed also that out of Canada's 4,000,000-odd children under 16 years of age 500,000 are undernourished, 250,000 suffered from defective hearing, 77,000 have weak or damaged hearts, 55,000 are victims of tuberculosis, 1,000 are wholly and 3,800 are partially blind.

Also that out of 26 leading countries of the world, only four had worse records of maternal death-rates than Canada.

Such revelations, as reported in the Toronto Daily Star, "to whose accuracy Dr. Gordon Jackson, Medical Officer of Health for Toronto, gives unequivocal endorsation, should be a source of natural humiliation which all classes should be anxious to remove."

Sir Edward Mellanby, secretary-general to the Medical Research Council of Great Britain, pointed out that diet is of first importance from a health standpoint. The health of Britain's poorer classes was exceedingly low—22,000 would-be recruits out of 58,000 for the British Army were rejected because they could not pass the physical examination.

"There is a great amount of stunted growth in all countries," he said, "stunted both physically and mentally. The poorer the person, the more likely he is to be stunted."

You will find the same condition in all of the so-called "civilized" countries. During the last 50 years in the U.S.A. the increase of Epilepsy has been 450%; Diabetes, 1800%; Bright's Disease, 650%; Anemia, 300%; Insanity, 400%; Heart Trouble, 300%; Cancer, 308%; and, while we have the distinction of raising the world's best hogs, we have 75% of the world's Sinus Trouble.

CHAPTER 5

GIVE US THIS DAY OUR DAILY BREAD

For almost two thousand years, Man has prayed, "Give Us This Day Our Daily Bread." In the olden days, bread was made from unleavened whole grain—very little if anything being discarded. It was veritably the "Staff of Life". Man still prays the same prayer, but what a difference in the article he receives! Instead of being called the staff of life, it might better be called the staff of death.

The wheat is now crushed, ground to a powder fineness, the best parts being separated from the grain and this "life" part saved for farm use—to make healthy poultry, cattle and other farm animals. The remainder is sifted through silk and then this lifeless flour is bleached with a poisonous chemical till it will not support the life of even a grub. A great many people, within the last few years, are beginning to wake up and realize that they are being robbed of these precious elements in the original flour, so certain synthetic vitamins have been added to this dead flour. This has been accompanied by a great deal of advertising, urging people to eat more of this bread so that they will be healthier. However, if you put a cockroach in a jar containing whole wheat flour and "enriched" flour you will find it will eat the whole wheat flour but will not touch the "enriched" product. Perhaps this is because he has not been able to read what the manufacturers say about the wonderful qualities of this flour. Every insect and animal has an innate intelligence or natural instinct for self preservation. As we grow farther away from Nature, we lose this instinct. Children have it to a certain extent; they love to get into the fresh growing vegetables in the garden, but they can hardly be forced to eat the boiled devitalized vegetables.

Take a piece of fresh white bread and squeeze it in your fist. It makes a doughy mass that, when eaten, clogs up even the healthiest bowels. White flour makes an excellent paste for sticking paper to the wall and is the only proper use for it.

The same thing applies to rice—the brown polishings, which are so valuable, are removed and only white starch remains. And sugar has met the same fate—the sugar beet or cane stalk being robbed of all its minerals and vitamins till only a concentrated sweetness remains.

The chief reasons for this refining process is that there will be little monetary loss to the parties concerned in the marketing of these products. Little consideration is given to the loss of health to the millions of consumers. More people are killed from refining and adulteration of foods than from all the wars put together.

Dr. Frederick F. Tisdall, of the Hospital for Sick Children and University of Toronto, Canada, in addressing the dietetic section of the American Hospital Association at the Automotive Building, stated that the cattle and livestock of Canada are fed much better than the people are, because breeders know that they must feed their animals properly to make money. As an example, he cited the case of wheat. Mankind eats white flour from which the vitamins and nine-tenths of the minerals have been extracted, while the cattlemen buy rich wheat germ and inner bran for their herds.

In speaking at North Toronto Collegiate, Dr. Tisdall showed a picture of a farmer's child proudly holding a champion chicken; the boy himself, however, was a victim of rickets. The farmer had applied sound scientific principles to the rearing of his chickens, but adequate attention had not been given to his own child although the right food was available.

Making money has become more or less of a science. Farm animals are raised for profit while the raising of children remains a haphazard proceeding. The average farmer is a student of dietetics as far as the feeding of livestock is concerned. He uses charts giving mineral and vitamin properties of feed, but the scientific knowledge of diet is not put into practice in the feeding of his family, and the result is seen in almost every home in the so-called civilized world.

Perhaps some day, when people wake up fully to what is taking place, or when the fever of commercialism shall have run its course, we shall again be able to pray, "Give Us This Day Our Daily Bread," and obtain something worth praying for.

CHAPTER 6

WHY DRINK RAW VEGETABLE JUICES?

The knowledge of proper nutrition in relation to the health of the body is becoming more and more generally recognized.

It has been known for a long time that there isn't a cell in the body that lasts longer than seven years, but few people realize that the majority of the cells do not live nearly as long as that; for example, you grow several fingernails in a year and flesh cells take only two years to be replaced.

Physiological chemists state that there is not a blood cell more than fourteen days old and that we rebuild a new heart every thirty days. Constant chemical changes are taking place within the cells of our bodies every second of the day and night; old worn out cells are discarded and new cells are replacing the old. "Thus," said Dr. W. Robert Keashen, a famous heart specialist, "if you select the proper chemical elements from your foods you may restore healthy cells to replace the old worn-out toxic ones and overcome many functional, and some organic or so-called incurable diseases of the heart."

The minerals and vitamins, so necessary for the rebuilding of healthy cells, are found in abundance in the natural foods, and yet most people are deficient in these precious elements.

There are several reasons for this:

1. Our food, such as grain, has been refined. In this process the germ and coarse parts, including most of the minerals and vitamins, have been removed.

2. When foods lack freshness they have lost much of their value.

3. Peeling or scraping vegetables removes a great deal of the minerals and vitamins which lie close to the surface.

4. Soaking vegetables in water leeches out much of their value.

5. Cooking, preserving and canning destroys a large amount of the mineral and vitamin content. Then, when food is boiled, a great deal more is lost in the water which is too often drained away.

As refined, cooked food forms the major (and in some cases, the entire) part of the diet of the average person, it is no wonder that, as the survey of the Ellen H. Richards' Institute indicates, only two persons out of 2,311 escape malnutrition, and we find the paradoxical situation of people starving to death on a full stomach.

A carrot left in your basement all winter can still be planted in the spring and it will grow. It is a live food. But that same carrot, if cooked, is dead food, and no power on earth will make it grow. What most people are doing is feeding live cells with dead food, and that is one of the reasons why degeneration sets in. Man, apparently, still remains the only animal who doesn't know how to feed himself. Cats and dogs get sick—they eat grass and get well. Their instincts are often safer than our intelligence. An elephant is the strangest animal in the world. He lives wholly on a vegetarian diet. We, of course, have not his digestive capacity but, through juices, we can tap his source of energy.

One of the major discoveries in nutritional research was that Nature never gives us isolated minerals and vitamins—she always gives them to us in combinations. Man probably does not comprehend one millionth of what still remains unknown in this field. We do know, however, that when we obtain these vital elements from the Master Chemist, we are obtaining, besides the known vitamins, also vitamins which have not yet been discovered.

Many people may be in apparent good health for years, yet sooner or later these continual borderline deficiencies lead to the eventual breakdown of health and the development of disease in some form. The greater the deficiency, the sooner will this breakdown occur.

Most of the necessary minerals and vitamins cannot be stored to any extent in the body and so must be replenished daily. So every day the diet should include raw foods, especially the green and yellow vegetables.

Some people object to eating raw salads. Some of the excuses they give are reasonable, others unreasonable. Perhaps the ones most frequently given are:

1. They don't like salads.

2. They have artificial dentures and cannot chew raw vegetables: very well.

3. They haven't time to eat a salad; it takes too long to chew it.

4. Their stomachs are sensitive and raw food causes distress.

5. Their powers of assimilation are weak and so they cannot digest the salads properly.

Far too few people realize the value of fresh raw vegetables in their daily diet. Eating raw vegetables occasionally does not do a great deal of good, as the body needs a daily supply of minerals and vitamins, and so they should get their raw vegetables in the form of raw vegetable juice.

It has been recently estimated that not more than 1% of raw vegetables are assimilated, as they are not masticated properly and the digestive juices cannot break up the cellulose.

It has always been considered that it was impossible to live on vegetable juice alone except in cases of short fasts, for it was believed that the body needed a certain amount of bulk for the proper functioning of the digestive tract. This idea has been confounded by Mrs. Moore Patalewa, a Russian-born woman living in England. This woman has lived for two years on nothing but juices, taking absolutely nothing more solid into her system than an occasional spoonful of honey. She takes from a pint to a quart of juices daily, engages in much more strenuous work than the average woman, is never sick or tired and expects to live to be 150 years old, she says. She turned from the civilized diet after a visit to India, where, in the Himalayas, like Dr. Robert McCarrison, she met men and women who were well over 100 years of age, but looked more like 35. Some had even cut their third set of teeth.

Another outstanding case which hit the headlines is that of Samuel Taylor of England, who at 80 has his third set of teeth. Two years ago he could barely hobble around and he was given only a few months to live. Now he walks daily 5 miles before breakfast and three times a week he walks 30 miles per day. He is becoming young and spry and his neighbors are all marvelling at the transformation. He finally told them it was all due to the fact that he started to drink a special brew his grandmother used to make, consisting of stinging nettles, dandelions, fresh green shoots, elderberry and red clover blossoms.

There are various reasons why a juicer is a MUST in every home:

1. Persons who have poor teeth, artificial dentures, or indeed, those that have no teeth at all, can take their raw vegetables in the form of juice.

2. A person who has no time to eat a proper dinner can get all the nourishment from a salad in the form of juice. It is quickly consumed and easily digested.

3. A person with stomach or intestinal ulcers cannot eat raw vegetables, yet he can drink carrot juice. There is no roughage to irritate and it is very soothing, healing and nourishing. To them, raw carrot juice is worth its weight in gold.

4. In the form of juice, a greater amount of vegetables can be taken into the system than could possibly be eaten. Only the cellulose is discarded. The juices, with all their minerals and vitamins, flood the body with minerals to build strong healthy cells. Thus the body is revitalized in an amazingly short time. One well-known Ontario surgeon prescribed as much as a gallon of raw carrot juice daily for one of his most serious cases. It would be an absolute impossibility to eat the amount of vegetables required to make this amount of juice.

5. The raw juices are a boon to invalids who have lost their appetite, as they can drink their nourishment without having to force food into an unwilling stomach.

6. Raw carrot juice is excellent for little babies and can be combined with milk without curdling. It is also good for growing children, as it contains the minerals and vitamins so necessary for health and growth. They will drink the delicious juice when it is sometimes impossible to coax them to eat their vegetables.

7. It is excellent for adolescent children, as it aids in the normal development of the glands and helps to avoid the pimply condition so usual at this period.

8. It is a great aid in strengthening the aged and in helping prevent the constipation and gall stones which are so closely related to soft refined foods and inactivity.

9. Above all, raw vegetable juice taken daily by young and old, healthy and ill, is a guarantee that the body is receiving its quota of building materials for all the trillions of cells of which the body is composed.

Most people drag themselves along, not realizing that, through proper diet and with the aid of an abundance of vegetable juices, they could just as well be strong and healthy and enjoying every minute of their trip through life.

However, it is becoming more and more widely known. Thousands of people today owe their health and even their very lives to the fact that they were made acquainted in time with the healing, revitalizing power of raw juices. Thousands of mothers have watched with thankfulness their poor sickly children transformed into strong, red cheeked boys and girls. Thousands of people who really struggled to get their daily work done now find their work easy and themselves with plenty of energy in the evening to enter again into social life.

CHAPTER 7

GENERAL RULES TO RECOVERY

The following chapters are suggestions only. There is within each person, an Innate Intelligence that can direct the healing or correction of any part of the body if one will only allow it to work unimpeded by obstructions.

Everyone possesses a certain amount of "ignorant education" which has to be forgotten. With all Man's vaunted "knowledge," he cannot put together one single tissue cell and make it live. Innate Intelligence, however, can put together four hundred billion cells, each in its proper place, and produce a baby in two hundred and eighty days.

One must first put himself in harmony with the Law of Nature and thus allow the Innate to function. This law has operated throughout all the centuries and will continue to operate for the good of each person if one will only allow it to do so.

In the various chapters of this book, the suggestions are based on the result of research, which data has been carefully gleaned from various reliable sources. They are suggestions only, but a great many people have found that following these suggestions has placed them more in harmony with the Law of Nature and the result has been more than they ever dreamed was possible. Follow Nature's Law, consume only what the body requires, think positive, constructive thoughts, and allow the Innate to direct the healing of the body.

Individuals differ, both in their determination to carry a plan to its conclusion and also in their opportunity for putting their plans into effect. This chapter will outline general rules to be followed, but these rules may have to be adjusted to the individual. If the rules can be followed in their entirety, results should be obtained more rapidly. Remember, if you want a perfect body, you will probably have to work hard to undo the ravages of years of wrong feeding, and the more serious the condition to be corrected, and the longer the body has been afflicted with the disease, the more difficult will this task be.

However, IT CAN BE DONE. Each person has been given a wonderful body and provided with all the materials, in the form of natural foods, to keep that body functioning properly; the only thing is the faith and determination to follow Nature's laws. "Put your hand in the hand of God" and go forward towards your goal. Faith and cheerfulness are your armor, and the natural foods are your weapons against disease. Fear, anxiety, hate, jealousy, envy, and such negative emotions are the allies of ill health, while hope, courage, cheerfulness and determination and such positive emotions will carry you forward to success. Hold that vision, follow Nature's laws and nothing can keep that vision from becoming reality.

However, don't think for a moment that the value of the juices and proper diet is merely psychological, as some scoffers may have you believe. It is not through a rat's belief or disbelief in the value of proper diet that he becomes ill when fed on deficiency rations and becomes well again when the missing minerals and vitamins are again added to these rations. Faith without works will not carry one very far along the road to health and one cannot easily become well unless he puts his knowledge of nutrition into effect. However, Man is an animal whose actions are influenced to a large extent by his thoughts, so use these thoughts to assist in the proper rebuilding of the body. This will be covered more fully in the chapter on "Nerves".

"There is but one disease—deficient drainage." This quotation from Sir William Arbuthnot Lane cannot be too strongly stressed. Before any disease can be conquered, the waste accumulations must be cleansed from the system, and the more quickly this is done, the sooner will the body be in a position to start its rebuilding program. "Cleanse the body of its wastes, feed it properly and the miracle is done," Sir William continued.

The quickest way of cleansing the body of its wastes is probably through the purge and then the fast. Directions for the purge are as follows:

THE PURGE:—(Note: NO ONE WITH APPENDICITIS OR INFLAMMATION OR ULCERS IN THE DIGESTIVE TRACT SHOULD ATTEMPT THE PURGE—IT IS MUCH BETTER FOR THEM TO PASS DIRECTLY TO THE FAST).

The purge is of untold value in most cases, as it speeds up the recovery tremendously. Almost miraculous results have been reported in so many cases,—fevers disappearing, pneumonia and hay fever subsiding, and a great many disease conditions responding almost immediately, simply because the accumulations of toxic poisons have been discarded from the body. The purge should last from one to three days, depending entirely upon the condition of the sufferer and how well he responds to this program.

Immediately upon arising, before dressing or increasing the circulation in any way through exercises, dissolve one tablespoonful of Epsom salts in half a glass of boiling water (distilled water should be used at all times in this purge if at all procurable). Add to this the juice of two lemons and fill the glass with water. Drink this and twenty minutes later take half a glassful of carrot and celery juice or citrus juice diluted with half a glass of distilled water. During the rest of the day, the juice and distilled water should be repeated every half hour. No food of any kind should be taken during the purge, or the value of the program will be lost, although if very hungry an orange or grapefruit may be had in the evening. During this period, Nature is housecleaning drastically, and in the process poisons which have probably been accumulating for months or even years are dumped out of their resting places to be eliminated, and these poisons naturally have a reaction on the body, sometimes causing violent headaches, nausea, and weakness. This, however, is only temporary, and should soon disappear once the poisons are eliminated, and then Nature will not be hindered in her task of rebuilding.

FASTING:—After the purge is finished, it is well

to continue for a few days on a liquid diet, sometimes called a fast, during which time nothing is taken except raw vegetable juices. This fast should last from one to five days, depending entirely upon the condition of the individual. As in the purge, weakness, headaches and dizziness are usually felt, but this is not alarming when one understands what is causing these reactions. Nothing but raw juices and distilled water should be taken. If in a cold climate, the water should be warmed a little before drinking. During this period, as in the purge, the cleansing process continues, and it is well to take an enema or high colonic every night to cleanse from the intestines the poisons being loosened from the various cells of the body, otherwise there will be reabsorption into the blood stream and little will be gained. If an enema is used, it should consist of warm water into which has been squeezed the juice of a lemon.

A day-a-week fast is recommended for anyone who cannot take a longer fast—in fact, it is an excellent thing for anyone to take whether sick or well, as it gives Nature a chance to get rid of the accumulations or acid poisons in the system, thus preventing future trouble.

For anyone who cannot take the purge, it is well to start with a natural laxative, the night before starting the fast.

During the fast as much of the raw juices may be taken as desired, the most pleasant combination being that of carrot and celery juice. This may be diluted half and half with distilled water for quicker absorption. If one finds it hard to live on the juices only, it is permissable to eat an orange or other raw, juice fruit occasionally.

One middle-aged man from Phoenix, Arizona, reported that he had been on the juices alone for fifteen days—taking absolutely nothing but the juices—and that on the fifteenth day he felt much stronger than when he began, the juices giving him an abundance of energy. His physical appearance had greatly improved, his eyes sparkled like diamonds. His wife, however, who had a very bad case of arthritis, had to break the fast at the end of five days, as the cleaning process caused a great deal of distress. Then, after eating for two or three days, she resumed the fasting. If one will follow this regime he will find that the periods of distress will gradually become less and less as the body regains its normal functioning.

BREAKING THE FAST:—In breaking the fast, eat a large raw salad, consisting of lettuce, and any combination of the following: carrots, celery, cabbage, onions, ripe tomatoes, cucumber, raw spinach, with either olive oil and lemon juice or plain. CHEW THIS THOROUGHLY. If a complete bowel movement is not had within two hours after eating this, drink a pint of flaxseed tea made from simmering four teaspoonfuls of flax seed in one quart of boiling water for about five minutes and then setting aside for an hour and strain. Then eat another raw salad. For the next two or three days, the meals should consist of raw fruits and vegetables—nothing else—with hot or cold water and juices to drink.

FOODS TO INCLUDE IN THE DIET:—The diet should consist almost entirely of fruits and vegetables, a little whole grain products, with a small amount of such foods as milk, cheese, eggs, nuts, fish or meat, unless otherwise advised under the chapter on the special diet in question. A yellow and green vegetable should be eaten every day, and it should be raw. Honey or raw sugar or molasses should always be used in place of white sugar, and lemon juice in place of vinegar.

FOODS TO EXCLUDE FROM THE DIET—"SUICIDE'S DELIGHTS":—The highly acid-forming foods which should be excluded from the diet are: All foods containing white sugar and white flour, rich preserves, candies, pickles, vinegar, condiments (pepper or other seasoning), alcoholic drinks, strong tea, coffee or cocoa, highly seasoned foods, and greasy or fried foods of any kind.

Gandhi, who had a great deal of experience in fasting, followed these rules:—

1. Conserve your energy, both physical and mental, from the very beginning.

2. Cease to think of food while you are fasting.

3. Have a warm sponge bath daily.

4. Take enemas regularly during the fast. You will be surprised at the impurities you will expel daily.

5. Sleep as much as possible in the open air.

6. Bathe in the morning sun. A sun bath and air bath is at least as great a purifier as a water bath.

7. Think of anything but the fast. Think of your Maker, and of your relation to Him and His other creations.

You will make discoveries that you may not have dreamed of.

Of course, Gandhi did not have the raw vegetable juices to drink. Most people who drink these juices find that they have more strength and energy than they have had at any time in their lives. The raw juices make it safe to go on a cleansing program, for they supply the necessary minerals and vitamins to feed the billions of little cells in the body. Dr. C. W. Cavanaugh, of Cornell, states, "There is only one disease, and that is malnutrition. All ailments and afflictions to which we may become heir are directly traceable to this major disease."

CHAPTER 8

THAT TIRED FEELING

"Here rests to fortune and to fame unknown
Some heart once pregnant with celestial fire;
Hands that the rod of Empire might have swayed,
Or waked to ecstacy the living lyre."
—Gray's Elegy.

How often have we felt within us the longing to do something great. We feel we have the ability, but simply lack the strength of body to carry it through! We are virtually slaves to a worn-out framework. And the tragedy is that Nature supplies us with everything to make a vibrant body, brimming over with the joy of living and eager for new tasks to conquer—but we lack the knowledge of how to use her gifts.

Fatigue has often been called "the great American disease." So many people are tired—just too tired to do the work in life they would like to do and that they know in their hearts they could do. So many people have success just within their grasp, but they are too tired to make that extra effort required. Nutritional efficiency often determines whether a person succeeds or fails in life. The better the nutrition the more chance we have of reaching a ripe old age with all our senses alert and with energy and capacity left for enjoying life.

Plants constitute our only direct method of conserving the energy which we continuously receive from the sun.

47

When Sir John Boyd Orr was in Canada lecturing under the auspicies of the Canadian Medical Association, he emphasized the effect of diet on mental as well as physical health.

He explained that, in a recent survey in Great Britain, over 25% of the women in some districts suffered from anemia due to the lack of iron in their diet. "These women were easily tired; they were listless, they were often melancholy," he said. And he continued, "An anemic woman is not usually a very pleasant person to live with."

He told of a woman doctor in England who made a special study of anemia in women. This lady doctor stated that when the anemic condition was overcome by the diet richer in iron, the women became much more cheerful and began to take more interest in life. They became neater and began to dress better. She said that what struck her was that many of them went out and bought new hats.

Sir John said, "I mention this because it is an illustration of the effect of health on our outlook on life. If we have perfect health we get a kick out of life. We are 100% alive. A healthy person is usually a cheerful person, full of the joy of living which accompanies health."

Lord Orr received the Nobel prize for his outstanding work in nutrition in its relation to world peace. He used this prize money (about $22,000) to further the promotion of peace and world government.

So many people these days are dragging themselves through life—no energy, no pep—just half alive! They have, usually, no definite pain, and so do little or nothing about their condition, for it is a regrettable fact that most people will do nothing till Nature prods them with the sharp spear of pain.

Anemia is caused by a failure to take into the system enough of the proper materials for Nature to build the red blood corpuscles. These red blood corpuscles act as little ships to carry the oxygen (which we breathe into the system) to the various parts of the body where it is unloaded. The oxygen then combines with the waste material to form carbon dioxide, which is carried to the lungs to be breathed out of the system. If there is an insufficient number of these little ships there will be a gradually increasing amount of waste accumulating in the body and the sufferer may slowly weaken and die. Any exertion breaks down more cells and causes a heating in the body which is the burning up of waste, forming more carbon-dioxide, which will further poison the system. Nature, in order to protect the body as much as possible, takes away from the anemic person the desire for exertion.

The symptoms of anemia are unmistakable; the sufferer is continually tired even in the morning upon arising; he has no ambition to get things done, and is often very irritable. Psychologists explain this as a sense of guilt, or failure, for not doing as much as he feels he should. Some anemic people do get a lot done, but only because this guilt or failure complex is so strong that they drive themselves mercilessly.

One of the most important things formerly advised in overcoming this anemic condition was the use of liver extracts, once considered a cure, but a high protein diet affects the kidneys, and so many of those "cured" of anemia died later of Bright's Disease. Hence this "cure" was not so favorably looked upon. It is, however, of the utmost importance that the diet is one that is rich in iron, but it is also imperative that this iron is obtained in the organic form—that is, the form found naturally in the vegetables and fruit. It is almost impossible to correct this condition through eating alone, for the vegetables are so bulky, and the stomach is so small. It is, therefore, vitally necessary to drink large quantities of raw vegetable juices in order to get a sufficient amount of the minerals and vitamins so necessary for Nature to use in the building of these red blood corpuscles. The combination of carrot, celery and beet juice has proved to be a seemingly miraculous help to so many people. The carrot, to build up the general health level; the celery for the nerves (and most anemic people have bad nerves); and the beet, for this wonderful vegetable contains practically everything to build up the blood and the heart.

If at all possible, it is best to start with a thorough cleansing. Follow the directions for cleansing as given under "General Directions." After the cleansing program, follow a diet consisting chiefly of fruits and vegetables, especially the green leafy vegetables. In season dandelion greens, spinach, romaine lettuce, Kale, chard, watercress, beet greens, cabbage (the green leaves) and green string beans, should be taken. And they should be raw, if at all possible, as cooking destroys so much of the value. Any of these may be juiced and taken

in combination with carrot juice or carrot and
celery juice.

Egg yolks are also high in iron and may be taken
up in the juice, discarding the white of the eggs.
Egg yolk may also be combined with a glass of
orange juice.

The diet may also include melons, pineapple,
prunes, raisins, oranges, tangerines, peaches, pears
and apricots. Also nuts or cheese or lean meats,
especially liver, kidneys, gizzard. Any bread eaten
should be of 100% whole wheat or rye. Chew your
food thoroughly, for often a person whose digestive system is in a weakened condition, absorbs
only a very small percentage of what is eaten.
Therefore chew every mouthful of food till it is
practically in a liquid form.

The sufferer should, if possible, spend at least
two hours daily out of doors in the sunshine. If
there is a lack of sunshine, some form of fish liver
oil should be taken to get the necessary Vitamin D.
One should not overexert himself, as it is important to build up and strengthen the body in every
way possible, but gentle exercise such as walking,
stretching and deep breathing are important, as it
stimulates circulation and thus more oxygen is
taken into the system. Remember, the reason the
red blood corpuscles are needed, is to enable more
oxygen to be absorbed, so plenty of fresh air is
necessary. Sleep and rest, too, are necessary. At
least two daily rest periods of about 15 minutes
each will help greatly. A warm bath should be
taken at night and a cool one upon arising. If
unable to take a cool bath, the entire body should

be rubbed briskly for three or four minutes with a dry rough towel. This will stimulate the circulation and bring the blood coursing through the veins.

But remember, the most important thing of all is to take into the system every day the materials needed by Nature to build red blood corpuscles. An anemic person will be surprised at the change in himself after even one month of the above program.

One woman in Ottawa, Canada, who had been very anemic for years, after following this program writes: "I have been enjoying such good health ever since I started taking the juices. Before I started taking the juices I had a hard time to do my own housework, and if I did one day's work, I would sure be sick the next, but not now. I have taken a daytime position in the civil service and still have plenty of energy left to do my house work at night." And at the time of starting on these juices, her husband, who was a mounted police at the Parliament Buildings there, was unable to work with neuritis in his shoulder. In three weeks he was back at work, with no more pain.

Another case worthy of note was a woman, staying at that time in Bellingham, Washington. She frequently had hemorrhages and once, after a particularly bad hemorrhage, felt as if her life blood had ebbed away and that she was almost dying. She suddenly thought of a case of Boysenberries she had on hand. She put them through the juicer and drank the liquid. In about fifteen minutes, she said, she felt life again pulsing through her veins and the color returned to her cheeks. She said it was an answer to prayer. God helps those who help themselves, and there is everything in Nature to build and heal the body.

They feed carrots to a race horse—it gives them lots of energy. Of course, a horse has a large stomach, but we can consume as many carrots as a horse can, if we throw away the roughage or cellulose and drink the raw juice which contains the valuable part of the carrot.

CHAPTER 9

THE HARDENING PROCESS

*High Blood Pressure and Hardening
of the Arteries*

This condition is most often found among the older or middle-aged, and has most distressing symptoms, such as dizziness, pounding in the head, headaches, and general feeling of nervousness. It is found more frequently among the overweight than among those of normal or subnormal weight, as the blood has to be pumped through a much greater area in the former case, thus putting a greater strain on the heart.

In high blood pressure, there is a thickening or contraction of the arteries, usually accompanied by hardening. The heart has to pump much harder in order to force the blood through the decreased blood vessels, so the name of high blood pressure is given to this condition. Because of the hardening of these arteries, they cannot expand as they should when the blood is being pumped through them, and occasionally one of the walls break and blood escapes. When this occurs a clot, or thrombus, as it is called, is formed. This clot may lodge in the brain, thus cutting off messages to parts of the body, the condition being known as a stroke, or, if a clot happens to lodge in the heart, it cuts off the free flow of the blood to or from the heart, causing a terrible spasm of pain, or even death itself.

A great deal of research has been carried on at the University of California, proving the relation of diet to health and disease. A report of the work of Doctor James F. Rinehart and Doctor Louis G. Greenburg, was published in the American Journal of Pathology.

Monkeys fed on a diet deprived of Vitamin B6, or Pyridoxine, for from five and a half to sixteen months, all developed hardening of the arteries. A control group of monkeys received Pyridoxine and did not develop this disease. The hardening of the arteries progressed much the same as in humans, the inner lining loosening and the cells multiplying and thus decreasing the size of the arteries, with the resultant condition which we know as high blood pressure. It took a relatively long time to create this condition, just as it does in humans.

This lack of Vitamin B6 is one of the causes of weakening of the walls of the arteries, but there are probably many causes. However, in all diseases, we find first, a weakening of the cells and next, waste deposits in those weakened cells. In recent years, it has been discovered that a certain waxy substance called cholesterol deposits on the inside of the blood vessels, which helps to make them thicken and harden. Deposits of calcium also has the same effect. Have you ever noticed in an arthritic, calcium always settles in the weakest part—where there has been a previous injury, perhaps.

As organic sodium tends to keep calcium in proper solution, it is very important that the diet consists of a great deal of the foods containing this element. After the calcium has settled, it is almost impossible to EAT enough of the sodium foods to do a great deal of good, as the stomach can hold only a small amount of the bulky vegetables; then, too, the vegetables have to be chewed, digested and absorbed before they are taken into the blood stream. In the form of raw vegetable juices, there is no chewing and practically no digestion required. Within fifteen minutes after drinking them, they are taken into the blood stream and carried to every cell in the body. Thus a strong solution is carried through the arteries and the organic minerals, direct from the live plants, somethimes accomplishing seeming miracles in taking back into solution the deposits along the walls of the arteries or veins. However, these juices must be entirely free from pulp, or hours may elapse before they are taken into the blood stream. Best results are also obtained when the juices are taken on an empty stomach. High blood pressure usually responds to a combination of carrot, celery and beet juice in a remarkably short time.

High Blood pressure is often found in connection with nephritis, gout, valvular diseases of the heart and in all those conditions which are the result of over-feeding combined with lack of exercise, or with worry. Meat eaters invariably have a higher blood pressure than vegetarians.

Summing up, the chief causes of this condition are:

1. The over-consumption of fats, starches, meats, and rich foods.

2. The use of stimulating drinks such as tea, coffee, alcohol.

3. Stimulating foods such as seasoned and spiced foods, tobacco and drugs.

4. A lack of the natural foods which contain the necessary elements to prevent the depositing of calcium and cholesterol in the arterial walls.

Through the process of breathing, oxygen is taken into the system. This oxygen combines with the waste matter to form carbon-dioxide. If we do not get rid of this waste matter, Nature attempts to increase the blood pressure to force the blood to the lungs to absorb more oxygen. In kidney diseases Nature raises the blood pressure so that more blood will be forced through the diminished blood vessels there, to clean out the accumulations of wastes. Thus we see how Nature is always trying to correct any condition which would interfere with the body's normal actions.

In order to assist Nature in her attempt to correct this condition, we must first help her in her task of cleansing the body of waste deposits. First, cleanse the body, then build up good healthy cells which can do their work of keeping the body functioning properly. A fast should be undertaken for from one to seven days, depending upon the severity of the case and upon the tolerance of the patient. During this time, nothing should be taken but the juices of fruits and vegetables, such as oranges, grapefruit, lemons, apples, a combination of carrot, celery, and beet and, if any water is used, it should be distilled.

Every night of the fast, an enema, consisting of warm water and the juice of half a lemon, should be taken to cleanse the body of the poisons and wastes which are being loosened by the action of the juices.

After the fast, the diet should consist of nothing but raw fruits and vegetables for at least two weeks longer. No starch, fat, or protein whatever, should be taken during this period. It will be astonishing to most people to note the results usually experienced in this length of time, but it is simply a matter of co-operating with Nature and assisting, instead of hindering, her efforts to help the body right itself.

After the restricted diet, other things may be added, the diet then consisting of the following: fruits and vegetables, both raw and cooked, raw fruit juices, raw vegetable juices in generous amounts, whole grain breads and cereals, a very little lean meat, fish, or fowl, wheat germ and beans. The wheat germ should be taken daily either in orange juice or added to the cereal after the cereal is cooked.

The following is a list of foods to be avoided: butter, cream, ice-cream, milk, fats, meat, egg yolk, lard, heart, liver, kidneys, sweet breads, oysters, crabs, shrimp, lobster, fish liver oils, fat meats such as bacon, pork, sausages, or gravies, chocolate or foods containing chocolate. A little margarine may be used in place of butter. Salt should be strictly limited. Tap water should be avoided, using distilled water instead. Sugars and starches must be cut to a minimum.

A hot Epsom salts bath, using 2 1/2 lbs. of commercial Epsom salts to the bath, should be taken nightly for the first week just before going to bed. Remain immersed in this bath for 15 minutes massaging every part of the body. This promotes circulation and perspiration (thus assisting Nature in the work of ridding the body of waste matter through the pores of the skin) and also relaxes the nerves. In severe cases where the patient cannot help himself, a plastic sheet should be placed on the bed and the patient wrapped in a cotton sheet wrung out of cold water, then in the plastic sheet. Place 3 or 4 hot water bottles around him and cover him well with blankets. This wet pack promotes elimination through the skin, relaxes the arterial tension and induces sleep. The patient should remain in the wet pack for several hours or all night if desired.

When able, a daily walk is excellent, gradually increasing the distance. Breathe deeply while walking, as this relaxes the nerves, and learn to put out of the mind all worries or destructive thoughts. Every afternoon, take a rest, picturing pleasant and relaxing scenes. Sometimes a cloth wrung out of cold water and placed on the forehead, will assist in putting all exciting thoughts out of the mind. Reading of good constructive books assists in keeping the mind cheerful.

A combination of carrot, beet and celery, with emphasis on the celery juice, is very beneficial. The drink should be made palatable so the patient may take copious amounts of it, taking at least two quarts daily. Garlic is helpful and may be added to the juice, or garlic capsules may be taken in addition to the juices.

When unable to get natural sunshine, Vitamin D should be taken through sun lamp treatments as the body cannot utilize the calcium except in the presence of Vitamin D.

There appeared in the Lewiston Tribune, Lewiston, Idaho, a report of a prominent Philadelphia heart specialist. Dr. Edward L. Bortz stated that the average person does not take care of himself. He takes too few baths, eats too much of the wrong kind of food and generally overstuffs, passes up exercise and doesn't bother to relax. He said that was what really kills them. They wear out their bodies 30 years too soon. Blood vessel breakdown causes four times as many deaths as cancer, and this means that people are just worn out, run down by neglect. Heart failure, strokes, high blood pressure, varicose veins, coronary thrombosis—all are variations of blood vessel breakdown. Dr. Bortz recommends health conservation or preventive medicine. He said, "The whole philosophy must be changed from curing people after they get sick to one of keeping them from getting sick at all." He said this should start right in the schools—in the kindergartens, if possible.

Dr. Bortz said, "The life span of the individual could be increased 30%; he could live to be 100 easily by correct living. Actually the life span today is no longer than in the days of Christ. In the

United States, the people are overfed. If Americans would cut down on eating 50% they would live longer and be healthier. The average person thinks that plenty of food gives him health. That's a mistake, mainly, because so much of today's food is fatty. Fat causes most blood vessel breakdown." Dr. Bortz, who is past president of the American Medical Association and chief of medical service at Lankenau hospitals, is recognized as an authority in this field. He said that health conservation should be one of the major projects in every community.

The response of high blood pressure to the use of juices and proper diet is becoming common knowledge. The first thing a modern doctor does now-a-days is to put a high blood pressure patient on a diet. The use of the raw juices usually speeds up the recovery tremendously. The following is a letter illustrating this:

"Before I commenced taking the juices I used to have such terrible dizzy spells, then I would feel weak for the rest of the day. The doctor said my blood pressure was terribly high, but would not tell me how high it was. I was putting on weight also. The neighbors didn't think I would follow the diet, but I lived on juices alone for four days. I didn't think at first that I could go without eating, for in the morning I used to always feel so weak if I didn't eat, but I found the juices satisfied me and I didn't get hungry and weak. I broke the fast after four days on the juices and ate only fruit and vegetables for two days. Since that time I have not had a dizzy spell and feel so much better. I have lost quite a lot of weight and the neighbors are remarking about it. I feel so much better now that I am very thankful that I started on the diet." Mrs. J. D. Kitchener, Ont.

Many other letters could be inserted here, but they would only duplicate what is stated in this one. High blood pressure is usually one of the quickest diseases to respond to proper diet and raw juices. Proper diet has also proved very beneficial in cases of paralysis due to a stroke. One Medical Doctor in Spokane put a nurse on a diet of raw vegetables, fruits and juices, when her whole side was thus paralyzed. She lived on this diet for one year, and by that time she had regained complete recovery of the affected parts. This was 20 years ago, and the nurse is still tending to her duties and living a very energetic life.

Arthritis and Rheumatic Conditions

Arthritis, that horrible crippler, is perhaps one of the most dreaded diseases known. More money is spent in trying to escape the painful torture of this ailment than on probably all the other diseases combined. This is due to the fact that arthritis seldom kills—it cripples and tortures its victims and finally renders many of them completely helpless, and yet allows them to live on and on in a veritable hell on earth.

Usually, when the sufferer feels the first symptom of arthritis, he is advised to have his teeth out. It matters little that he may have a splendid set of teeth—out they come. No relief. Then out come the tonsils. Still no relief. Then probably hundreds or even thousands of dollars are spent on injections, serums, electrical and other treatments too numerous to mention. He is indeed fortunate if he finally realizes the truth—that he is, himself, causing the arthritic condition and that the only way that he can ever expect help is through a reversal of his wrong eating habits.

The modern food diet of cooked, demineralized, "devitamized" food, accompanied by poor elimination, produces a great deal of acid poisons which bathe the cells of the body, causing pain, swelling and inflammation. When accompanied by a lack of organic sodium, calcium tends to settle in the various parts of the system, for sodium is the mineral which helps to keep calcium in proper solution so the body can utilize it. When this calcium settles in the joints, we have the condition known as arthritis, when in the gall bladder or kidneys, we have gall stones or kidney stones, and when in the walls of the arteries, high blood pressure or hardening of the arteries. Thus it will readily be seen how very important is the consumption of foods rich in organic sodium. We find this mineral in abundance in celery and cucumbers, but it is impossible to eat enough to do a great deal of good. However, when the juice of these vegetables are taken on an empty stomach, within 15 minutes they are carried to every cell in the body. It is a strong solution racing through the blood stream and can do wonders in taking the calcium back into solution. When this is accomplished the arthritis disappears. Vitamin D, the sunshine vitamin, is also necessary, for without this vitamin we cannot utilize the calcium in the body. Also Vitamin E is necessary, for this vitamin is a muscle lubricator. This is especially needed in muscular rheumatism.

Vegetable juices are very alkaline and so raise the alkalinity of the body. This relieves inflammation and swelling and so simple rheumatism or neuritis often respond very quickly. It takes longer to clear up the calcium deposits, but they, too, should quickly respond, and recovery can be expected if the proper minerals are taken into the system and a health program followed.

In gout, there are lime deposits in the joints of the feet, the big toe being affected first. There are also lime deposits in the skin of the ear and sometimes in other parts of the system, but it is most noticeable in the feet. It used to be called the "Rich Man's Disease," as it is the result of rich foods, often accompanied by the drinking of alcoholic beverages and an unbalanced diet. There is usually a great deal of pain and inflammation.

Bursitis, or Housemaid's Knee, is a condition where there is inflammation of the sac under the knee cap. This sac contains fluid and, due to the fever and inflammation, more fluid collects there, causing pressure on the nerves around the knees, creating a great deal of pain. An injury may cause the trouble in the first place, or continual pressure such as induced when scrubbing floors, but the inflammation is aggravated by a highly acid condition. Anything causing pressure must be discontinued and the program as outlined for arthritis followed.

Lumbago is a rheumatic condition in the lumbar,

or lower area of the back. Muscular rheumatism, or fibrositis, is well known to almost everyone on the so-called "civilized" diet. However, the chief sufferers are usually those who engage in rather strenuous work, standing or sitting in one position, where the blood does not have a chance to circulate properly.

Some years ago a dentist attended a lecture on Raw Juice Therapy, in a small town in Eastern Canada. This dentist was brought to the hall in a wheel chair and was the most pitiful object imaginable. Every joint in his body was affected with arthritis, even his jaws being in such a condition that he could no longer chew any food. For a long time he managed to push bits of food between his teeth, roll it around with his tongue and swallow it, but for some time he had not been able to do even this, and was living on liquids which he sipped through a straw. He was nothing but skin and bone and was literally starving to death. When he saw the vegetable juices, his eyes lit up. "At least that is nourishment I can take," he said, and immediately started on a program in which he drank great quantities of carrot and celery juice daily, besides taking sun baths practically every day. The report two and half years later was that the doctor was back doing all his own dental work with only a trace of arthritis between his shoulders.

Here we see Nature at her best. As it was impossible for him to eat solids, he responded much faster than if he was daily putting into his system loads of waste matter which would have to be eliminated.

The program for correcting arthritic or rheumatic conditions should begin with a thorough cleansing as outlined under "General Rules," accompanied by a fast. This fast should last as long as possible, the duration depending upon the patient. Patients with weak hearts should be under the care of a doctor who understands fasting and the relation of food to the health of the body, if at all possible. If this is impossible, then the patient must be his own doctor and analyze himself as much as possible. Remember, if an animal becomes sick, he stops eating. After breaking the fast, the diet should consist chiefly of fruits, non-starchy vegetables (both raw and cooked), very little whole grain cereal, and some protein such as meat, eggs or meat substitute. No bread should be eaten. The cereal should be cooked thin and then a handful of wheat germs should be added and served immediately without further cooking. The wheat germ should be obtained fresh weekly from some reliable feed and seed store and kept in a cold place to prevent deterioration. If unable to take sun baths, Vitamin D should be taken in the form of capsules or Cod Liver Oil or Halibut Liver Oil. However, this vitamin should never be taken until after sundown. The diet should be somewhat as follows:

About fifteen minutes before breakfast, drink a glass of water which contains the juice of half a lemon. This should be unsweetened. BREAK-FAST—Cereal cooked as outlined above, may be served with cream and sweetened with honey or raw sugar; Or—fresh raw fruits may be eaten instead, the wheat germ being taken during the day alone or with orange juice. DINNER—This meal should consist of a salad made of the following: 1

tbsp. honey, 2 tbsp. hot water, 1 tbsp. cream, 1 tbsp. raw oatmeal, 1 tbsp. ground nuts, 2 medium sized apples chopped fine, juice of half a lemon. Mix well and serve. As much as desired of this salad may be taken, but no other food at this meal. SUPPER—Cooked vegetables and a raw salad. The vegetables should be cooked in such a manner as to preserve as much as possible of their value. They should never be peeled. Meat, eggs, fish, or meat substitute may be had. For dessert, either fresh fruit, dates, figs, or a baked apple sweetened with raw or brown sugar or honey. FOODS TO AVOID: Milk, cheese, cottage cheese, salt, spices, vinegar, white sugar, white rice, white flour, or any foods containing these. DISTILLED WATER SHOULD BE USED IN PLACE OF TAP WATER. ESPECIALLY IF THE WATER IS CHLORINATED. However, if enough juices are taken, it will not be necessary to drink water at all. At least two quarts of juices should be taken daily.

A combination of carrot and celery juice has been found of great value, but cucumber or the juice of swiss chard or Chinese cabbage may be substituted for the celery juice, when available. If the circulation is very bad, as in the case of so many arthritics, a little beet juice may be added.

A friction bath should be taken every morning, using a rough towel wrung out of cold water, rubbing the entire body briskly until the skin is pink. This procedure should take only about five minutes. Massage is very helpful—in fact, there should always be some motion, as calcium settles faster when the joints are still. The patient can usually do a great deal of exercising himself.

Crocheting is good exercise where the joints of the arms and hands are affected. Other similar exercises can be thought of by the patient. He can also do some of the massaging, which consists of working the flesh as deeply as possible around the ends of the bones, never on the bones. If unable to help himself, the massaging should be done for him; however, care should be taken to allow no rough handling of the affected parts, as this will only make matters worse.

Three nights a week, a hot bath should be taken, consisting of hot water into which Epsom salts has been added. Dissolve 2 1/2 pounds of Epsom salts in the bath water as hot as can be borne by the patient. Remain immersed for 15 minutes, massaging the entire body thoroughly, then dry quickly, and go directly to bed, being careful not to get chilled.

If unable to take a complete bath, a handful of Epsom salts should be added to a bowl of hot water and towels, wrung out of this solution, placed around the affected parts. Apply this hot towel for 5 minutes, then apply a towel wrung out of cold water. Repeat this several times. This could be done daily or even several times daily where there is a great deal of pain. After this application a light massage may be followed with fingers dipped in olive oil. This will help to promote better circulation, aiding in breaking up of the calcium deposits around the joints.

As in all cases of ill health, fresh air and sunshine and a cheerful determination are important. Worry is a rider who spurs many people to their graves.

It is of the utmost importance that properly fitting shoes be worn—many cases of hip pains disappear entirely when shoes are corrected. Look at the heels. If the heels are worn on one side they should AT ONCE be rebuilt, as this puts a strain on the entire leg muscles and this also affects the sciatic nerve.

CHAPTER 10

DIGESTIVE TROUBLES

Ulcers and Colitis

Raw vegetable juices are worth their weight in gold to anyone suffering from these conditions.

What else is there that an ulcer patient can take? Milk and cream? The Journal of the American Medical Association reported cases, living on a milk and cream diet, developing beri-beri and scurvy, for this diet is lacking in essential minerals and vitamins to maintain the health of the individual. Citrus fruits and their juices usually cause a great deal of distress and so are avoided. Dr. H. A. Warren of the Peter Brent Hospital in Boston, found that nine out of ten persons obtaining treatment for ulcers had less than the normal amount of Vitamin C in their blood. So it is of utmost importance that ulcer patients include an extra amount of the foods containing this vitamin in their daily diets. Cabbage juice is very high in this vitamin, as well as containing Vitamin U, which prevents the development of peptic ulcers.

Dr. Garnet Cheney of Stanford University Medical School, San Francisco, reports the very favorable results he obtained with thirteen patients. Each patient was given one quart of cabbage juice, squeezed from fresh raw cabbages. Celery juice also contains this anti-peptic ulcer vitamin, so a few of the patients who found cabbage juice hard to take, were allowed to combine it, using 75 percent cabbage juice with 25 percent celery juice. They were allowed to season it with a little tomato juice and to eat crackers with the juice. The juice was kept well chilled and served five times a day to the patients, but was not allowed to be kept overnight, as it was then found to be less palatable. No medicines were used, although where constipation was present, a little milk of magnesia was allowed. The diet consisted of milk, eggs, cooked vegetables, such as carrots, peas, green beans, beets, squash, potatoes; cooked fruits such as peaches, apples, apricots, cherries, or pears; bread made from whole grains, finely milled, also cereals made from the same sources; a small amount of butter, postum, sugar, honey, jelly and clear syrups. Excluded from the diet was pork, fried foods, fats, ice cream, and roughage such as skins and seeds. The patients were allowed to eat between meals if they desired.

In the test on the thirteen patients, some with long-standing cases of ulcers, the ulcers disappeared in eleven cases in from six to nine days. One case required 23 days to heal. In the other case, the ulcer disappeared in eight days, leaving a bumplike deformity. Seven of these ulcers were in the duodenum and the others were in the stomach.

Vitamin U is contained in a great many of the fresh green vegetables and cereal grasses as well as in certain vegetable fats, but it is easily destroyed by heat. As most people live almost entirely upon cooked foods, it is no wonder that there are so many cases of ulcers. After the ulcer has developed, it is impossible to eat raw vegetables on account of the roughage, but they are easily taken in the form of raw juices.

Another diet which has helped a great many back to health and freedom from digestive worries and is very easy to take is as follows:

A glass of flaxseed tea and carrot juice is taken alternately every two hours. (Flaxseed tea is made by pouring one pint of boiling water over two tablespoons of flaxseed and simmering for three or four minutes. Let stand for one hour, then strain.) For two days the program should be: 1 glass flaxseed tea—one hour later, a glass of carrot juice—one hour later, a glass of flaxseed tea, etc. No food should be eaten. Each night an enema consisting of warm water with the juice of half a lemon, should be taken. Then the following diet is suggested:

BREAKFAST: Carrot juice, stewed fruit (with the skins removed) sweetened with honey or brown sugar. A glass of flaxseed tea.

LUNCH: Carrot juice and celery juice. Steamed or waterless-cooked vegetables, milk or buttermilk.

SUPPER: Steamed or waterless-cook vegetables, whole-wheat toast (dry), saturated with olive oil. Chew each piece into consistency of apple butter before swallowing. A glass of carrot and celery juice.

Drink carrot and celery juice any time during the day. A yolk of an egg may be added to this drink if desired.

Follow this diet for a week or until all pain disappears. Then gradually add to the diet egg yolks, cottage cheese, honey, broiled lamb chops and chicken. Do not use orange or grapefruit juice or raw vegetables for a while, as they may cause more irritation.

Drink flaxseed tea night and morning. When the condition is greatly improved, add fruit juices, eat raw fruit, peeled, also finely grated salads. Remember to chew every mouthful *thoroughly*. After four or five months, when all pain has disappeared, go on a three-day cleansing diet, taking nothing but three meals a day of fresh ripe juicy fruit, but no bananas, or dried, stewed or tinned fruits. Take an enema each night. This cleansing program will thoroughly cleanse the system, but should not be undertaken until the ulcerated condition is corrected.

No salt, white sugar, pepper or spices should be taken, and no fried food of any kind. Vegetables are best steamed or waterless-cooked, as most of the minerals and vitamins are lost through boiling.

If the bowels do not move, take an enema—never a harsh laxative. Be sure that there is complete evacuation every day, using the squat position for bowel evacuation.

Take a daily walk and breathe deeply. Worry or sense of frustration can actually bring on an attack of indigestion. Read the chapter on "Nerves." Try to relax more. Don't give your stomach so much work to do. Chew your food thoroughly—simply by eating slower and chewing the food thoroughly, a great deal of the torments of indigestion can be avoided. Some people have obtained wonderful results in mild cases of indigestion simply by chewing the raw celery, spitting out the fibers, and swallowing the juice.

The use of hot water bottles or electric pads over the painful area will help to allay the distress.

The treatment is the same for both ulcers and colitis. The following are two letters from women, one of whom had ulcers of the stomach and the other a terrible case of colitis. They both followed the same regime and were both delighted and grateful for the results obtained.

"For some time now I have been going to write about the results obtained from the carrot juice diet, which I tried for stomach ulcers. As far as I can make out and from recent X-rays there is no sign of the ulcer or even a scar in my stomach. It took exactly four months to accomplish this on your diet (after four years of medical treatment)." Mrs. G. C., Peterborough, Ont.

"This is to tell you of the results which I got from the juices and diet which I have followed since the first of February.

"I had mucous colitis for two years and suffered so much I thought I was going crazy. I had been in the hospital half a dozen times having my stomach washed out. I had hypos and had 17 X-rays. Finally five doctors said they couldn't do anything more for me. I was so weak they all said I would have to eat, but I couldn't eat. I was continually passing mucous and blood and was getting weaker all the time. My bed was brought downstairs, for I couldn't climb the stairs very well. I couldn't stand having company come in and I didn't want to go out anywhere.

"Finally my daughters got Dr. Henry, and he said I should start these juices. I started the next day on your diet for mucous colitis, taking the carrot juice and flaxseed tea, and I have been following the diet strictly ever since. The results have been greater than I ever dreamed was possible.

"I have practically no pain now at all and my nerves are all right again. I am sleeping good and feel so strong I am going out with my daughters everywhere. Really I feel like a new woman. I couldn't have believed it possible if someone had told me the results I would have obtained in five months. I am not passing any mucous or blood now at all and my bowels are perfectly normal again. I am certainly glad I found out about this before it was too late.

"My daughter who had arthritis in the shoulder has started to take the juice and feels so much better already".—Mrs. B.B., London, Ont.

Gall Bladder Trouble

As the gall bladder plays a large part in the digestion of foods and malfunctioning of the gall bladder upsets the digestion to such a remarkable degree, it must be included in this section.

It has been estimated that 40 percent of all women over 45 years of age develop gall stones, and Dr. Clendenning cites the fact, proved by autopsies, that 90 percent of all people over 80 have gall stones.

Some years ago, Dr. Charles C. Higgins of the Crile Clinic in Cleveland, announced that a painless diet could be used in combatting kidney and bladder stones. He told of experiments on albino rats in biochemical laboratories where diets deficient in Vitamin A produced stones. He said these stones were dissolved after feeding diets rich in Vitamin A. Then, he reported, eighteen humans were put on a diet rich in Vitamin A. Some of these had had operations for stones and the diet prevented new stones from forming (something that often happens) or where new stones had begun to form, the diet quickly dissolved them. In others who had stones and who had not had operations, remarkable results were observed: In two patients, the stones had completely disappeared within four months and in one where the stone completely filled one kidney, the stone had entirely dissolved in six months.

All green and yellow vegetables and fruits are high in Vitamin A, and a good general rule to follow is:—the deeper the color usually denotes the more Vitamin A content. It is very hard to eat a great deal of the bulky vegetables in order to get a sufficient amount of Vitamin A, but these vegetables can be taken in the form of raw vegetable juice, and usually very fast results are observed. Carrot juice is very rich in this vitamin as well as in most of the other vitamins and minerals, and this juice, being delicious, can be taken in abundance, therefore, it is of utmost importance in the diet where a gall stone or kidney stone is present. Celery juice, with its rich sodium content is used to hasten the dissolving process, and a small amount of raw beet juice is added to help carry the waste matter from the bowels. Spinach juice is also excellent, but is not so pleasant to take.

In regards to gall bladder trouble, the same suggestions apply as for liver trouble. The diet should be very light, consisting chiefly of raw, juicy fruits for breakfast, a large combination salad for dinner, and another salad and some cooked vegetables (if desired) for supper. A little hard, dry, whole wheat toast may be had with the salads. Distilled water should always be used in place of tap water in cases of stones, or vegetable and fruit juices, only, for beverages.

In severe cases, take a warm water enema twice daily, using the juice of half a lemon in the water. If there is pain over the gall bladder area, hot compresses may be applied several times daily to relive the distress. A hot Epsom salts bath consisting of one pound of Epsom salts to the bath of hot water (no soap), should be taken several times weekly before retiring. Remain immersed in the hot water for from 15 to 20 minutes, massaging the entire body, then dry and go directly to bed.

The patient should go to the toilet every morning upon rising and also within half an hour after each meal and concentrate upon bowel elimination, as it is important that the bowels be kept free so there will be no reabsorption of waste matter into the blood stream to further poison the gall bladder. If unable to have a natural action, it is important that an enema be used.

In severe cases, where stones are present, excellent results have been obtained where the following was taken:

2 oz. Corn Oil, 2 oz. Peanut Oil, 2 oz. Olive Oil, juice of half a lemon. After drinking this, the patient lies on his right side for 10 minutes with a heating pad over the liver area. This should be taken in the evening. In the morning take a saline solution.

The juice combinations which have proved very effective are:—2 quarts of carrot juice combined with a pint of celery juice and the juice of the three large beets. Cucumber juice or the juice of swiss chard may be substituted for the celery juice when obtainable. Always make the combination palatable with the addition of enough carrot juice.

A letter from a follower of these natural methods writes: "For many years I suffered with gall stones. For days at a time, I had to have hypodermics to get any relief at all, then the attack would wear off only to recur again in a few weeks. I finally reached the point where everything I ate made me roll on the floor in agony. My family and friends finally decided something would have to be done, and an operation was planned for the following week. About that time, this wonderful little book fell into my hands and changed the whole tenor of my life. I followed the suggestions for Gall Bladder Trouble and in a very short time I was completely cured. Today, after nearly two years, I do not know what it is to have any gall bladder distress. When I think of all the mixtures I swallowed in endeavoring to find relief, this natural method seems like a miracle."

In summing up the diet, the outstanding things to remember are:

1. No eggs.

2. No bananas.

3. No chocolate, cocoa or alcoholic drinks.

4. No grease, gravies, fried foods, pork, fats.

5. No cream, ice cream, milk or butter.

6. Use plenty of lemons, grapefruits, oranges, or all other fresh raw juicy fruits.

7. If any water is used, it should be distilled.

8. Use plenty of raw green and yellow vegetables—especially in the form of juice.

CHAPTER 11

ELIMINATION

Constipation

Constipation is considered the cause of a great many of the ills to which human flesh is heir to, but did you ever stop to wonder what causes constipation? This condition, like every other condition of ill health, is merely the result of wrong diet, and putting off Nature's urge to evacuate. The only way to correct constipation, like the only way to correct every other wrong condition, is the reversal of factors which caused it.

Constipation is almost always the direct result of wrong diet—the consuming of soft, refined, devitalized foodless foods. If you squeeze a handful of fresh white bread, what do you obtain? A doughy mass that would be almost impossible for even the strongest bowel muscles to force along through the many feet of intestines. On the other hand, it is just as wrong to eat a lot of rough bran or other harsh cellulose. Whole natural foods, such as whole grains, raw salads, properly cooked vegetables, and fresh juicy fruits will tend to raise the health level of the entire body and also to provide a natural bulk on which the intestinal muscles can operate.

Another great cause of constipation, however, must not be overlooked, and this is the taking of purgatives and laxatives in the endeavor to "cure" the constipation. The irritation of these drugs causes the colon to contract and, if used repeatedly, the over-stimulation tends to exhaust the muscles. The continual taking of purgatives is like whipping a tired horse to make it keep trotting. The taking of mineral oil coats the intestinal wall and prevents the absorption of minerals and vitamins, especially Vitamin A.

A constipated person is often listless and lacks ambition. His mind is usually less active. He may have headaches, anemia, liver and gall bladder trouble or kidney trouble. Often the constipation is blamed for these ailments, but the real cause of all ailments is improper diet and improper care of the body.

The diet should be corrected, and when this is done, we often find that the bowels begin to function more normally at once, but oftener it takes a little while, especially if the muscles of the intestines are so exhausted that they have not been in the habit of working naturally for some time. So, if these muscles need assistance for the time being, an enema or a natural laxative may be taken. If the enema is taken, take only as much water as is absolutely essential to start the fecal matter. Often only a cupful is needed before the bowels start moving.

The enema should consist of warm water and the juice of half a lemon. If a natural laxative is used the amount taken should be decreased each night till the bowels move without it. Teach the muscles to act of their own accord. This action is encouraged by having regular periods of going to the toilet. The time may be arranged by the individual himself, but usually within half an hour after eating is found best, also immediately after arising in the morning. The squat position should be used, placing a stool or box under the feet if necessary. The body will soon adjust itself and regular evacuations will be had. Deep breathing and other simple exercises, such as stretching and bending, will help to strenghten the abdominal muscles and should be taken each morning; then a brisk rub with a rough towel to stimulate circulation.

Certain foods are more laxative than others, prunes and figs being excellent. In using these, simply cover with boiling water and leave to soak all night. Do not cook or sweeten. Several prunes should be taken each morning or during the day if desired.

The breakfast should consist of fresh ripe juicy fruit, but if very constipated, a large bowl of finely grated cabbage and apple—nothing else, should be had. If cereal is used, it should be of whole grain (made thin) and, when cooked, a handful of fresh wheat germ added and served immediately without further heating. Wheat germ should be obtained fresh weekly from a health food store and kept in a cold place.

The dinner should consist of the following:—1 tbsp. honey, 2 tbsp. hot water, 2 tbsp. raw oatmeal, 1 tbsp. wheat germ, 2 medium-sized apples grated fine, 1 tbsp. grated nuts, juice of half a lemon. Mix all together and serve. For best results, nothing more should be used during this meal, but as much as desired may be eaten.

The evening meal should consist of several cooked non-starchy vegetables, a salad of green leafy vegetables, and either cottage cheese, meat, meat substitute, fish, eggs, or nuts.

IT IS OF UTMOST IMPORTANCE THAT THE FOOD BE CHEWED THOROUGHLY.

Beet juice and also spinach juice are both very laxative. These may be combined with carrot and celery juice and taken any time during the day. If very constipated add several beets or one cup of spinach juice to one quart of this combination, but decrease the amount of beet juice or spinach juice if found too laxative. Sometimes celery juice, which tends to relax the nerves, is all that is required in overcoming the constipated condition.

One woman from Kitchener, Ontario, wrote as follows:

"I have had wonderful results from the vegetable juices. I have been taking them regularly for about a month and I certainly feel different.

"I had been constipated for about forty years. It seems as if the nerves of my abdomen would cramp and knot and I would have a dull ache there. I knew something was wrong. I had pains that seemed like appendix pains but they have all gone now. I feel so good now that I feel like running at my work. My nerves are quiet and I am telling others how much better I am feeling and how Nature has helped me.

"I wouldn't think of going to bed without my celery juice."

Appendicitis

The cause of appendicitis is inevitably linked up with bowel sluggishness and is the direct outcome of a toxic bowel condition and the taking of purgatives and laxatives. Any extensive accumulation of waste matter in the colon over a period of time can lead to the development of appendicitis. Removal of the appendix does not alter this toxic condition—in fact, constipation is usually worse after this operation than before and adhesions frequently occur.

The cure of appendicitis is simply a matter of cleansing and purifying the whole of the digestive system, but this cannot be accomplished through the use of drugs. If there is any pain in the abdominal region or any sense of nausea, it is particularly dangerous to take laxative into the system—that laxative may be your death warrant. Stop immediately the intake of all foods and liquids, although tiny sips of cool water with a little lemon juice may be taken if very thirsty. Watch an animal—if he becomes sick through eating too much of man's devitalized food, he stops eating till Nature has corrected the effects of wrong feeding. Cold compresses may be placed over the painful area several times daily, and an enema, consisting of one pint of warm water with a little lemon juice in it, can be given daily, or several times daily for the first two or three days to cleanse the lower bowel, but only if it can be taken comfortably, not otherwise. NO LAXATIVE OF ANY KIND SHOULD BE TAKEN.

About the third day, the condition should have eased sufficiently so a full enema could be taken without distress. This consists of about three pints of warm water with the juice of half a lemon. This should be repeated daily thereafter until pain and inflammation has subsided. From the third day onward, fruit and vegetable juices may be taken, also water if desired.

As soon as all pain has disappeared, which should be about the fifth day, the patient may break the fast and then start on a program of healthful eating, the diet consisting mostly of raw fruit, vegetables (both raw and cooked), and either meat or meat substitute. Starch and sugar have a constipating effect, and so these should be avoided till the bowel action has become so corrected that regular evacuations are being had. If a proper diet is followed, constipation should not last long but, until the bowels are working normally, enemas may be taken nightly—never laxatives. If this program is followed there should be no recurrence of the appendix trouble.

Dr. William Howard Hay, M.D., in his book, "The New Health Era," tells of his work in connection with appendicitis. In over 400 cases, every case cleared up without recourse to surgery, even though nineteen of these were cases where the appendix had been ruptured before being brought to his attention. Contrast this with the fact that almost every patient dies if an operation is performed after the appendix has been ruptured.

Nature seals up the abessed area until such time as it can be drained into the colon and when Man breaks into this sealed-off area, thus permitting the abscess to drain into the abdominal cavity, he can only expect disaster.

A combination of carrot, celery and beet juice is excellent for the cleansing and healing of the colon, also carrot and spinach. In fact, all the raw vegetable juices are purifiers of the colon, the carrot juice being the most healing. About two quarts daily should be taken. This should be taken only after the acute symptoms have subsided and liquids are allowed. Foods should be combined properly, referring frequently to the Radiant Health Food Chart till the knowledge of proper combinations are easily recognized.

Kidney Trouble

The kidneys have a tremendous amount of work to do, for they, like the liver, filter the blood. The filtered wastes are then excreted in the form of urine. The more wastes in the blood stream, the greater is the work put upon the kidneys, and if this strain is continued, they will eventually break down. Overwork of the kidneys is caused by several wrong habits:—

1. The consumption of too much meat. This creates excess uric acid and may produce, in time, an inflammation known as Bright's Disease.

2. The eating of too much of the starch foods, or even too much of any kind of food, as anything that cannot be used by the body is poison to the

body and must be gotten rid of if health is to prevail.

3. The use of too much table salt puts a great strain on the kidneys, as they work very hard in trying to rid the body of this irritant. If the excess salt cannot be excreted, nature attempts to protect the body from harm by causing more water to be retained in the tissues to keep this salt in solution. This water accumulates in such parts as the ankles, the abdomen, the upper arms, and sometimes in the upper eyelids, the condition being known as dropsy.

4. A constipated condition allows absorption from the small intestines into the blood and lymph stream of an extra amount of waste poisons which put more strain on the liver and kidneys.

It will thus be seen that anything that causes injury to any part of the body will affect the kidneys, and pus or trouble anywhere may show up in the urine, as well as in the blood. As overwork or strain on the kidneys causes them to break down the only way to correct the condition is to reverse the causes, i.e., by stopping the intake of such things as are causing the overwork or strain and by cleansing the system of the poisons which are already present.

Omit entirely from the diet, for the time being, such irritants and stimulants as: meat, salt, spices, alcohol, tea, coffee, cocoa, etc. Decrease to a minimum starches, sugars, and even meat substitutes. The diet should consist chiefly of yellow and green vegetables and fruits and their juices, and the majority of this should be taken raw.

Constipation MUST be cleared up. This will be corrected by proper diet but may take some time if the condition is of long standing. In the meantime a mild herbal laxative should be used, or an enema consisting of warm water and the juice of half a lemon.

Begin the diet with a 3-day fast on vegetable juices and water. Every 2 hours from the time you arise till you retire at night, drink an 8 oz. glass of juice, sipping slowly. On the hours between, drink a glass of pure distilled water. If one has to get up at night to urinate, do not drink any liquids within 4 hours of retiring. This cleansing program will permit the elimination of poisons in all the tissues of the body, and so is of great value for even a well person to undertake occasionally. Break this fast as advised in "General Directions" and then start this program: First thing in the morning, either citrus juice or a combination of carrot, celery and parsley juice may be had. Then half an hour later, the following:

BREAKFAST: Fresh ripe juicy fruit in season. (If working, one or two coddled eggs may be taken in addition to the fruit). Such fruits as prunes, black figs, or raisins may also be had. This fruit should not be cooked, but should be covered with boiling water at night and allowed to soak till morning. No sugar should be added.

MIDDAY MEAL: This meal consists of either of the following: Fruits, such as oranges, grapefruit or grapes; or a large raw salad made of green and yellow vegetables and cottage cheese—no salad dressing.

EVENING MEAL: This meal consists of a meat substitute such as a soy-bean preparation, etc., one or two non-starchy vegetables such as string beans, asparagus, spinach, turnips, beets, parsnips, etc. (all cooked without salt); a salad of any of the following, or all together as desired—carrots, lettuce, tomatoes, celery, ripe olives, parsley. No dressing except a little lemon juice and olive oil if desired.

This may seem like a drastic diet, but the closer it is followed, the quicker will be the results obtained. Some obtain results from merely omitting from their normal diet such things as salt, meat, alcohol, tea, coffee, and cutting down on starches and sugars, and by consuming two quarts of vegetable juices daily, but better results are obtained, especially in severe cases, if the above is followed strictly.

The hot and cold Sitz-baths are of great value in assisting the kidneys back to proper functioning.

In connection with kidney stones, read the article in connection with Vitamin A and kidney stones as related under Gall Bladder Trouble, as the causes of these are very closely related.

Kidney trouble usually responds very quickly to proper diet, and sometimes in an amazingly short period of time. One man who had terribly swollen ankles, reported the swelling gone in one week. Other cases are very similar, some responding more quickly than others but all receiving great benefits. William Howard Hay, M.D., in his book, "What Price Health?" tells of his own case. He was dying from Bright's Disease, with high blood pressure, and a dilated heart, yet at the end of three months of proper diet he was again able to run long distances without distress, his weight decreased from 225 lbs, to 175 lbs. and he felt younger and stronger than he had for many years.

The Skin

The skin not only acts as a covering for the body, but also as a means of elimination of wastes and as a temperature control. There is within the body, a thermostat which causes the pores to open to allow perspiration to escape when the body temperature becomes too high. This perspiration, evaporating, causes a cooling of the body. Through the pores of the skin, each day, pass large quantities of toxic wastes. This can be readily seen in cases of jaundice. The poisons from the liver are yellow in color and, as a great deal of these poisons are eliminated through the pores of the skin, this yellowish tint is sometimes very noticeable.

Anything that affects the health of the body as a whole will naturally affect the skin. In constipation, the blood stream becomes laden with an excess of these toxic wastes, and nature attempts to eliminate them through the pores. This is one of the reasons for the much-publicized "B. O.", and using a medication which merely stops these pores can be very harmful. Sometimes this poisonous waste forms little pustules or scales, the condition being known as pimples, eczema, psoriasis, etc., and the only effective way to rid the skin of these irritating conditions is by a thorough cleansing of the body, both inside and out.

Vitamin A is especially needed by the skin, for without this vitamin, the skin cannot be healthy and smooth and firm. In severe cases of a Vitamin A deficiency there is a horny, dry condition, sometimes known as "toad-skin". If there is a lack of circulation the pores often become clogged with waste matter, causing blackheads. The use of salves or ointments will only further clog up these pores and thus make the condition worse. As carrot juice is exceptionally high in Vitamin A, it should be used in quantitites and, as beet juice tends to promote better circulation as well as being a laxative, it should be added to the carrot juice.

The patient should go on a cleansing program, taking a short period of purging and then a fast, during which time nothing is taken except distilled water and fruit and vegetable juices. Then for a few days, fresh juicy fruits should be added to the liquid diet. Then the diet should be a natural one, avoiding concentrated sugars and starches, fats and meats, strong tea, coffee, cream, ice cream, alcoholic drinks, pickles, condiments and fried foods of all kinds. Chocolate, soda fountain drinks, pastries, cheese and sweets are also to be shunned.

To aid in correcting a condition of pimples, drink a glassful of water with the juice of half a lemon first thing in the morning. Then wash the face in hot water, then with cold water. Next rub the affected parts with the inside of the lemon, then with the outside of the lemon. Wring a face cloth out of luke warm water and press on these affected parts. Allow the face to dry in the air so the lemon will remain in the skin.

Keep your hands and finger nails scrupulously clean. Never pick or squeeze the pimples, as this only bruises the healthy cells around the affected ones and makes the condition worse. Never allow the use of X-rays on the skin. It may do irreparable damage. If at all constipated, an enema should be taken nightly till the change to a more natural diet corrects the bowel sluggishness.

Two or three hot Epsom salts baths weekly will help to promote better circulation and also rid the body of a great deal of waste matter through opening the pores of the skin.

Plenty of fresh air, sunshine and rest should be had, and the mind should be kept calm. Your mind can make you ill, and this is shown very plainly in the skin. If a person becomes angry or excited, notice how the color of the skin changes. According to John A. Schindler, M.D., chief Physician of the Monroe, Wisconsin Clinic, "One third of all skin diseases treated by dermatologists are produced by blood vessels in the skin reacting to anxiety, worry, disgust, and so on. Each time one becomes upset serum is squeezed through the walls of the blood vessels and into the skin. The tissues become thickened with this serum. Finally this serum is pushed up through the surface of the skin, where it becomes scaly, crusty and the patient has neuro-dermatitis."

If the health level of the body is kept up through

proper diet, the nerves are not easily disturbed. Lettuce and celery are especially good for the nerves, and this is probably why so many people with skin troubles of all kinds, when taking these juices, respond so quickly, even in cases where the cleansing program is not carried out as advised. However, for a beautiful skin, it is well to cleanse the system first and then eat only what nature demands, avoiding the foods that create a toxic condition in which the nerves are easily disturbed. The reward is far greater than any little sacrifice, not only in a clear healthy youthful skin, but also in renewed health and vigor.

For eczema or psoriasis the same health program must be followed if the body is to be rid of these skin irritations.

Psoriasis is caused by a disturbance of fat metabolism according to Burger's functional test. He showed that a great many severe cases were corrected by following a diet low in fats. This has also been very helpful in eczema cases. All fatty meat such as mutton, pork, bacon, goose, duck, and fat meat of any kind should be ommitted from the diet. Also all fatty fish, such as salmon, carp, etc.; all cream, ice-cream, cream cheese, oils, butter, margarine, etc.; whole milk or buttermilk; all cakes, cookies, pastries of any kind, should be strictly forbidden.

There must be supplied, in the diet, all the minerals and vitamins which nature needs to build a strong, healthy body, and it is essential that this diet includes sufficient amount of Vitamin A, which is found in all green and yellow vegetables.

Sometimes the results are obtained so quickly that it seems miraculous, but it is simply that nature does the correction if she receives enough of the proper materials to work with.

Dr. Robert Jackson of Toronto, Canada, wrote: "To show what seemingly insignificant food changes will do, I cite a baby case seen some fifteen years ago. Weight six pounds at birth, only eight pounds at eleven months. Had rash diagnosed as 'infantile eczema,' in charge of a specialist. Not bathed for months, and never slept continuously for half an hour, or let anyone else sleep. I made only one slight food change, added four table-spoonsful of vegetable juices to its day's feedings. Three mornings later the grandmother phoned me to know if the baby was 'sleeping away.' Been sleeping fourteen hours—but she was only making up for lost sleep. Baths resumed, ointments discontinued. Immediately took on flesh and is now one of Toronto's loveliest fifteen-year-olds. The simple change added necessary minerals to the blood, destroyed acid-toxic irritants that had left the body via the skin, irritating it, and simultaneously child was vitalized—made resistant."

Cancer

As Sir William Arbuthnot Lane has said, "Cancer is created by poisons in our bodies through the food we eat. Nobody need have cancer who will take the trouble to avoid it." In the correction of this condition, the diet should be strictly vegetarian—no meat or eggs or breads should be taken. It is important that the body be rid of its impurities, for cancer is a scavenger which lives on waste matter, and the only way to get rid of it is by starving it out. Cancer cannot live in healthy cells. The diet should consist of raw fruits and raw vegetables and their juices if one is to get quick results. Many have reported results with merely changing their diet to a more natural one and the intake of quantities of carrot juice, but in very serious cases, it is important that drastic steps be taken at once.

It is best to start with a purge as outlined in the chapter "General Rules." Then a juice diet consisting of fruit and vegetable juices (raw) should be followed as long as possible, and nothing eaten whatever. If any water is taken it should be distilled. Better results will be obtained if this juice diet is followed for a long period of time, but the length of time will depend entirely upon the individual—some can follow this sort of treatment for longer periods than others. Remember, cancer is a deep-seated disease, and only drastic remedies will get results. That is, cleansing and rebuilding. Carrot, celery, and lettuce juice, or even carrot juice alone is excellent, as this is the healing juice. As much as desired may be consumed, but at least two quarts a day should be taken—more if possible.

Periods of exclusive juice diet may be alternated with periods of raw food diet, using particularly raw grated carrot and apples. Oranges and grapefruit may be used in any quantities. Grapes also are excellent, in fact, an exclusive grape diet for a while has given excellent results. Begin this with a short period of two or three days on nothing but raw grape juice, taking enemas daily to cleanse from the system the poisons loosened by the

juices. Then, after this juice diet, eat nothing but
grapes, using the following procedure: The first
thing in the morning, drink one or two large glasses
of distilled water, then every two hours from 8
a.m. till 8 p.m. eat one to three ounces of grapes.
This quantity is gradually increased till double this
amount is being consumed. Follow this program
for about two or three weeks. Later buttermilk or
sour milk may be had for supper instead of grapes.
After two or three weeks of this, a raw diet should
be followed, consisting of green salad foods, raw
vegetables of all kinds (except potatoes), nuts,
dates, honey. Finally, after full recovery, one
should follow a natural diet to prevent recurrence
of trouble, the best diet being fruit for breakfast, a
cooked vegetable dinner and a salad supper, using
meat in moderation.

The reason grapes get the results they do is
because they have great dissolving qualities and
their valuable iron content helps to build up the
blood. However, if the poisons are dissolved without being eliminated, trouble results. So it is much
better to use the carrot juice and distilled water for
a time before attempting the "grape cure." Carrot
juice not only heals, but it contains all the minerals
and vitamins to build good healthy cells and
tissues. Vegetable juices and distilled water should
be taken for as long as 21 days at a time if at all
possible. Here is a program followed by one lady
who obtained results beyond the greatest expectations of herself and family:

Two glasses of distilled water were taken upon
arising, then a glass of carrot juice every 2 hours,
alternating with carrot and spinach juice. This was

followed for a few days, then a glass of juice every hour, alternating the carrot juice with the carrot and spinach juice. This was continued for 21 days, then grapes were added to the diet, eating as much of the grapes as desired as well as drinking the vegetable juices. Then, very gradually, raw fruit and vegetables were added to the diet, also flaked nuts and honey. If she felt ill after taking any new food, she stopped eating and went back on juices for a few days. She says: "Don't become discouraged no matter how many times you have to return to the juices—you cannot lose if you keep fighting with Nature's remedies."

It may be hard to follow this diet, as the cancer seems to crave the dead, demineralized foods the same as a smoker craves tobacco, but do not give in—you must starve the cancer cells while building up good healthy cells, and the craving will grow less and less as time goes by.

It is of greatest importance that the bowels be kept perfectly clean. This may be accomplished by enemas, high colonics, or a natural herbal laxative.

Remember, if you provide the proper materials for the rebuilding of the body—in a form in which the body can assimilate—there is a power within you which can work seeming miracles.

CHAPTER 12

HEALTHY GLANDS

The Liver

In all cases of diabetes, anemia and gall bladder trouble, the liver should be suspected of mal-functioning, as there is very close association between the liver and these various ailments.

The liver is absolutely necessary to life. An animal lives only a few hours after having its liver removed, although it will live a little longer if glucose is injected into its veins. Thus it will be seen that the liver helps to maintain the normal level of sugar in the blood. Therefore, in all cases of diabetes, the cleansing and rebuilding of the liver is of utmost importance.

Any condition that involves the spleen also involves the liver, for whenever there is enlargement of the spleen, it will be found that the liver is also enlarged, thus in any case of anemia, the liver should be thoroughly cleansed.

Gall bladder trouble is very closely connected with an impure liver, and so in any bilious condition or wherever gall stones or inflammation of the gall bladder is suspected, cleanse the liver.

The digested food, absorbed through the small intestines, is carried to the liver. There, all nutritive material is filtered and allowed to pass into the blood stream, while harmful material is taken by the bile to the gall bladder and from there into the duodenum, where it is again carried to the small intestines. If the bowels are working properly, the waste matter should be carried to the large bowel and evacuated, but if constipation is present, waste matter may again be absorbed into the blood stream and carried to the liver.

The liver, even with the best diet, has a tremendous work to do, and sometimes gets clogged up with body wastes resulting from the over-consumption of the dead foods which are being continually eaten. Then, when a bilious headache occurs one usually asks for something to stimulate the liver so it will work harder, instead of trying to lighten its load. This is very much like whipping a tired horse to make it work harder instead of letting it rest and giving it lighter work. So the sensible thing to do is to lighten the work of the liver. This is best done by taking into the body only such foods as can be easily digested and which will leave the least end-wastes to be cleansed from the system.

There is a great deficiency of the Vitamin B Complex in the diet of civilized man, and this deficiency greatly affects the functioning of the liver. Fatty degeneration of the liver is directly associated with this deficiency. Vitamin B Complex is found in the organs of animals—the liver, kidneys, etc., in whole grains, and in vegetables, particularly the green leafy ones, and in yeast.

Vitamins C and K are both necessary, especially in cases of enlarged livers. Vitamin C is found in abundance in citrus fruit, tomatoes, green peppers, cabbage, as well as in most fruits and vegetables. Vitamin K is found in meat organs such as liver and kidneys, as well as in alfalfa, grass, and blackstrap molasses.

Chlorine is a mineral which is necessary for the cleansing of the liver and gall bladder, and is found in abundance in celery, beets, cucumbers, lettuce, endive, carrots, and radishes. Sulphur is a liver activator, and a cleanser, stimulating the flow of bile. It is found in most fruits and vegetables, but particularly in cabbage, onions, garlic, watercress, leeks, radishes, spinach, and egg yolk. Sodium is necessary to prevent such hardening processes as gall stones and kidney stones, and is found in celery, cucumbers, beets, dandelion leaves, carrots, lettuce, spinach, and apples, as well as in most other raw vegetables.

It will readily be seen that the diet should consist chiefly of the above-mentioned foods: fruits, vegetables (mostly raw), a little whole grain cereal (but very little) and, if desired, such meats as liver and kidneys, or cottage cheese and eggs. All starches, sugars and fats should be strictly avoided.

The diet should start with a juice fast, for from 3 to 5 days or longer, depending upon the condition of the sufferer and how well he stands the fast. During this time nothing should be taken but distilled water and the juice of raw fruits and vegetables. Celery juice should form an important place in this juice diet, also a combination of carrot and celery juice. Beet juice may be combined with the latter or taken with tomato juice, either raw or canned, to make it palatable (the tomato juice being merely a vehicle for the beet juice). Beet juice should never be taken alone except in small quantities, as it is a very powerful cleanser. Apple juice, cabbage juice, or the juice of any of the above-mentioned vegetables may be taken. By using different combinations, more may be consumed and it is easier to continue for a longer period on the juice fast.

After the juice fast, continue for the next three days drinking juices and eating oranges—as many as desired. Then add to the diet, vegetables (both raw and cooked), organ meats, cottage cheese, egg yolk, small amounts of whole grain cereal and wheat germ. No fried foods should be taken, and very little oil of any kind—even in salad dressing. Olive oil is best; a little butter may be had, but very little. No salt, alcoholic drinks, spiced or rich foods of any kind should be taken.

It is very important that the bowels be kept clean. Even on a fast, the daily enema should be resorted to, to cleanse the system of the impurities loosened by the juices.

Plenty of fresh air, rest, and sunshine should be had if at all possible. And a certain amount of bending and stretching exercises, unless these cause pain, should be undertaken, as they promote circulation to the liver, thus helping to cleanse out the impurities. Practice laughing. "A merry heart doeth good like a medicine" was no light saying. When you laugh, the action shakes and massages the liver and helps to make it function normally.

For ulcers of the liver, it would be best to continue to live entirely on juices for as long as possible, even up to three weeks or more. This should correct the condition quicker than anything else. If one finds it hard to continue fasting, he should return to eating, but try again and again to live for a few days on the juices alone. Remember, if one wants health, he will have to work for it. Everything is bought and paid for with a price. If one wishes to live on the rich foodless foods, he pays for the "pleasure" with his health. The cost is too high. A little determination to obtain health and the giving up of the old way of living and eating is richly rewarded.

Daily baths should be taken. It is best to take a warm bath in the evening before retiring and either a cool bath or a brisk rub with a dry coarse towel in the morning to promote better circulation.

At least two quarts of raw vegetable juices should be taken daily.

One woman who started on the above program had a liver so enlarged that her side appeared almost deformed, yet in six weeks time, the liver was back to its normal size and the "hump" across the one side had disappeared. Besides this, her whole outlook on life, and her general health and energy had wonderfully changed for the better. The liver usually responds very quickly to proper care.

When starting on a cleansing program, it frequently happens that the patient turns very yellow. If he did not understand what was happening, he might be tempted to discontinue the treatment, thinking that the juices were doing harm. The yellow color is caused from the poisons being flushed out of the liver to be eliminated from the system. As Nature eliminates a great deal of poisons through the pores of the skin, it is only natural that the skin would appear yellow. Have you ever seen anyone with jaundice? How yellow the skin is! This yellow color is not caused by the yellow carrot juice, for the sufferer probably has not been drinking juices of any kind. It is simply the yellow poisons from the liver. So, if you turn yellow after following this program, continue with the juices and thank your lucky stars that you are eliminating enough of the poisons from the liver to make you yellow. After the poisons have been eliminated, and the liver is again functioning normally, the yellow color will disappear and you should have a wonderful complexion.

The Pancreas—Diabetes

One hundred years ago, we consumed about four pounds of white sugar each, per year. Today, in one insidious form or another, we consume one hundred and eighteen pounds each per year. While this is not the only cause, it is a contributing cause, and statistics show that diabetes has increased 1800% in the last fifty years. Besides this, it is well known that there are a great many people who have this ailment but who are unaware of the fact. The American Diabetes Association in New York stated that, according to their statistics, there are an estimated 2,000,000 persons in the United States with diabetes who do not know that they have the disease.

Some of the easily recognized symptoms are excessive thirst and excessive urination. Suspicion of diabetes is proved or disproved by a test of the urine and the blood. When the pancreas becomes too weak to make up its digestive juice, called insulin, the sugar and starches in the diet are not digested and the sugar is thrown off into the urine and excreted from the body. The starchy foods turn to sugar in the process of digestion in the mouth when acted upon by a digestive juice called saliva. Sugar is needed by the body for fuel, and without it the body grows weak. By taking insulin the diabetic is enabled to digest and use the sugars and thus regain strength, but as long as insulin is being taken, there is usually nothing done to strengthen or build up the pancreas. It is just the same with constipation, as long as laxatives are taken every day, the bowels never will learn to function of their own accord, but will gradually lose all initiative. It is an important rule that any part of the body that is not used, will die. You have noticed this in connection with the muscular part of the body; it is the same elsewhere. So, you should try to encourage the pancreas to work for itself. This is best done by first easing its work by cutting down on the sugar and starch foods, and also by taking into the system the natural foods containing the necessary minerals and vitamins to build up good healthy cells and tissues, not only in the pancreas but also in the liver and all the other parts of the digestive tract.

Formerly the cause of the trouble was placed solely on a breakdown in the functioning of the Isle of Langerhans, a part of the pancreas where the insulin is manufactured, but more recently it has been discovered that urinary sugar can be caused by a malfunctioning of other organs, especially the liver, the thyroid and the adrenals, and perhaps by a breakdown of other organs or glands. It is, therefore, of great importance that the health level of the entire body be raised through proper diet. Nothing seems to succeed in this connection faster than the use of raw vegetable juices. It has worked seeming miracles in so many cases that it precludes the possibility of chance. Certain plants contain a natural insulin, and these should form a prominent part of the diet. The vegetables which should be used in abundance are cabbage, brussell sprouts, string beans, celery, carrot, and any of the green leafy vegetables. At least two quarts of the combination of any of these juices may be taken daily.

The only real correction of this condition is by cleansing the system and rebuilding the cells. The patient should first detoxicate as described in "General Rules". During this period, nothing should be taken except distilled water and raw juices, adding later raw fruits and vegetables which should form the major part of the diet. Since most diabetics are constipated, it is necessary at first, to use a thorough enema daily—even twice daily where necessary—to rid the body of its accumulation of debris, till such time as returning vitality will ensure natural evacuations from the colon.

The usual diabetic diet consists of far too much proteins and fats, as these tend to increase the acidity of the body. And, as sugar and starch foods cannot be used till the pancreatic function is restored, these, too, should be greatly decreased or eliminated as far as possible from the diet. This leaves only the salad vegetables and fresh acid fruits, steamed or baked non-starchy vegetables, milk, buttermilk, and vegetable juices. But this type of diet should soon restore the body to proper functioning. The patient will do better if this fruit-milk-vegetable diet is adhered to for long periods and will even gain weight if he is underweight. Studies of the blood should show a steady decline in sugar till, in a few months at longest, it should show a normal content.

If insulin is taken, it should be decreased as the patient needs it less, till at the end of two months it may not be needed any longer. However, if insulin is to be discontinued, it is of paramount importance that the diet include great quantities of natural foods containing the minerals and vitamins so necessary to the building of good healthy cells and tissues.

Dr. Michael Somogyi, biochemist of the Jewish Hospital of St. Louis, stated that 99% of adults can get along without insulin and that the others may need only a small amount. He further stated that the use of too much insulin can be dangerous, poisoning a diabetic and making him chronically ill through a chemical tug-of-war in his body. His report was made public on the eve of the society's 116th national meeting, and was reported in the Seattle Post-Intelligencer of Sept. 19th, 1949.

Dr. Arthur Vogelsang, of London, Ontario, found that Vitamin E was of great help in diabetic conditions as well as heart cases. Many cases treated for heart trouble, where diabetes was also present, found that, after a few months, insulin could be discontinued entirely, some obtaining outstanding results about four days after the high Vitamin E was begun.

Fresh air, sunshine, rest, and freedom from worry are essential, as these place one more in harmony with Nature's healing powers. Exercise helps to burn up blood sugar, so only mild exercise, especially walking, should be taken, the amount depending entirely upon the strength of the patient.

A combination of carrot, celery, and parsley juice with the juice of either string bean, cabbage or brussel sprouts, is recommended, using the carrot and celery in about equal proportions, or even one-third carrot and two-thirds celery. It is best to start with a small amount, about one large glassful the first day, gradually increasing the amount taken, until about two quarts per day are being consumed.

The Thyroid—Goiter

When the thyroid becomes so enlarged that it is readily seen or felt, it is known as a goiter. The most common cause of this enlargement is due to lack of iodine in the diet.

There are certain regions known as "Goiter belts", where the soil is deficient in this mineral and more people have this trouble.

Salmon and trout raised in hatcheries in a crowded state where there was a lack of iodine, suffered greatly from goiter, but these goiters disappeared when the fish were fed hashed sea food, which was rich in iodine.

In the Yellowstone River Valley, where there is a deficiency of iodine in the soil, there was a loss of about one million young pigs besides a great number of calves, colts and lambs each year from goiter, but when potasium iodine was added to the diet of pregnant sows there was no further loss due to goiter among their litters.

When iodine was lacking, a great many pigs were born dead and many others died shortly after birth. They were born with no hair and with great enlargement of the thyroid.

Salt from the mines used to contain iodine but, due to the usual "refinements" of civilization, it was made "pure", and the prevalence of goiter resulted. Sea water and sea foods are rich in iodine and people along the coast very seldom have goiters. Foods usually containing iodine are: Kelp, lobster, fresh cod, gray shrimp, scallops, herring, as well as artichokes, tomatoes, cucumbers, asparagus, carrots, potatoes, kidney beans, green beans, white cabbage, Irish moss, mushrooms, garlic, leek, lettuce, watercress, oranges, apples, lemons, pineapple, bananas, strawberries, whole wheat, rye, oatmeal, and nuts.

Of course the bowels should be kept regular and only natural foods consumed to lower the toxic condition of the body. Only by a thorough cleansing and rebuilding can the thyroid gland be restored to proper functioning. Follow the suggest-

ions as given in "General Directions." An excellent
way to proceed is as follows:—

Every other day the patient should go on a liquid
diet consisting of nothing but hot and cold distilled
water and fruit and vegetable juices. On the days
on which he is not on this liquid diet, raw tomatoes and cucumbers (nothing else) may be eaten,
and the beverage already mentioned. This should
be continued till definite results are are obtained.

The enema and Epsom salts bath should be taken
daily to cleanse the body, and a health program of
walking, fresh air, relaxing, and thinking of quiet
constructive thoughts should be undertaken, as
these will help enormously in restoring the body to
proper functioning.

Until the condition is entirely corrected, the diet
should consist almost entirely of raw fruits and
vegetables and their juices, some cooked vegetables, very little meat or other protein food, some
lobsters or other sea food, and a very little whole
wheat bread. The less sugar and starches consumed,
the quicker will be the results obtained.

A cold pack placed on the throat before retiring
is excellent local treatment. There should be about
five minutes of gentle massage before placing it and
after taking it off in the morning. To make the
cold pack, wring a wash cloth out of very cold
water. Fold and place over the goiter, then cover
with a piece of plastic material to retain the
moisture and to keep the bedding dry.

Deep breathing, brisk walking and a few simple

exercises should be taken daily and, if constipated, the chapter on this ailment should be read and put into practice.

The juice combination recommended is that of carrot, celery and watercress. When unable to obtain watercress, parsley may be substituted. At least two quarts daily should be consumed.

A kelp product of compressed seaweed could be used with advantage in connection with this diet. This may be obtained from a health food store.

Prostate Gland Trouble

The diet should be strictly a vegetarian one—no meat or eggs should be allowed. In fact, the closer the diet is composed solely of raw fruits and vegetables and their juices the quicker will results be obtained.

It is best to start with the purge as outlined in "General Directions." Then vegetable and fruit juices should be taken—nothing else—for as long as possible. Quicker results should be obtained if this cleansing program can be carried out for two or three weeks at a time, but the length of time depends entirely upon the individual—some being able to stand a longer period on this cleansing diet than others. Carrot, celery and some of the tops of carrot should be used, at least two quarts daily being taken.

Periods of exclusive juice diet should be followed by periods where the juice is accompanied by raw fruits and vegetables in salad form, using raw turnips every day. Oranges may be had in any quantities—also grapefruit. Grapes, too, are excellent—in fact, an exclusive grape diet for a while has been reported to have excellent results in very far advanced cases. Begin with a short fast on nothing but grape juice, then add grapes to the diet, eating 2 or 3 ounces of grapes every two hours from 8:00 A.M. to 8:00 P.M. After a few days of this gradually increase the amount of grapes taken. During this period, it is important that the bowels be kept clean with frequent enemas. In fact, all during the course of the treatment, this is extremely important. Instead of an enema, a natural laxative may be used. The grape diet may be alternated with a raw carrot diet, eating nothing but finely grated carrots and drinking an abundance of carrot juice. In fact, if unable to obtain grapes, this procedure of raw grated carrots and carrot juice should be followed. While on the grape juice diet, it is advisable to drink one or two large glasses of distilled water with lemon juice, unsweetened, first thing in the morning. This could very well be done also while on the raw grapes. Later sour milk or buttermilk may be used for supper instead of the grapes. After this, a raw diet of salads should be used until the trouble is cleared up. No milk, tea, coffee, cocoa or alcoholic drinks are allowed.

A warm bath should be had each evening and a brisk rub with a towel, wrung out of cold water, in the morning. At least once a day a Sitz-bath should be taken. This is done by placing two tubs side by side, the one containing about 4 or 5 inches of hot water and the other containing about the same amount of cold water. Sit in the hot water about five minutes then in the cold water about one minute. Repeat the procedure about four times, then go directly to bed.

At night, about three or four times a week, the hot bath should contain about 5 pounds of Epsom salts—no soap. Remain immersed in this water for about 20 minutes, having the water as hot as can be comfortably borne. Then dry and go directly to bed.

Hot and cold compresses, or fomentations, should be applied several times daily to the parts between the legs. A piece of cloth folded and wrung out of hot water should be applied about 3 minutes. Repeat three times, then finish with a cloth wrung out of cold water.

Simple exercises, especially bending and stretching, should be taken daily. The patient should drink as little fluids as possible after 6 o'clock. Fresh air, plenty of sleep and rest are important.

CHAPTER 13

CIRCULATORY TROUBLES

The Heart

"During the war years, heart disease killed six times as many Americans as were killed in action on the world's battle fronts," according to a report by David D. Rulstein, medical director of the American Heart Association.

Dr. E. V. Shute and Dr. A. Vogelsang of London, Ontario, and Dr. Wilfred Shute of Guelph, Ontario, have done great work in the use of Vitamin E in connection with heart trouble, the best results being obtained with coronary and rheumatic types of heart disease, although results were also being obtained with hypertensive cases. One man, who had been confined to bed for a long time, was up again after two weeks treatment with Vitamin E.

Vitamin E is one of the vitamins which is usually lacking in the diet of the individual. It is present in wheat germ, and wheat germ oil,. apple seeds, lettuce, and in most natural green plants and vegetables. In the early spring a rat will get into a bin of apples and split the apples open to get at the lifegiving seeds inside. Vitamin E, besides being necessary for the sex glands, is also a muscle lubricant, and the heart, being a very active muscle, suffers if this vitamin is not furnished in the diet. It is far more important to prevent damage to the heart than to wait for the trouble to start.

It is very important in all heart cases to avoid indigestion and allied ailments, for such troubles tend to affect the heart very much through pressure caused by gas. It is therefore always best to eat sparingly and to leave the table feeling that you could easily have eaten more. It is never wise to eat a meal late at night. Let the last meal be at least three hours before retiring. Avoid all white flour products, refined cereals, milk puddings and other mushy foods; avoid sugar in all its forms, condiments, pickles, sauces, etc., all fried food and, if possible, use eggs, cheese, nuts, or meat substitutes in place of meat in the diet. In any event, do not use much meat. Smoking should be cut to a minimum or, better still, cut out entirely. Avoid also the drinking of tea, coffee, alcohol or other stimulating beverages.

Quicker results will be obtained if the patient goes on a fast, but sometimes the heart is too weak to take care of the mass of waste poisons that is being loosened by the fasting process. It is, therefore, better to go a little slower and, in some cases, to leave out the fasting—at least till the heart is stronger. If able, however, the fasting as outlined under "General Directions" will obtain quicker results. The more a diet approaches a fruit and vegetable base, the cleaner will be the blood stream and the sooner will the heart be strengthened.

If constipated, for the first few nights of the treatment the bowels should be cleansed by means of an enema consisting of warm water and the juice of half a lemon. Do not take harsh laxatives. When the bowels begin to function normally of their own accord, discontinue the enema. In the mornings, a dry friction rub with a coarse towel, rubbing the entire body briskly for about five minutes to stimulate circulation, will be found very valuable. At night a warm water bath will be found relaxing. It is a mistake to think that heart sufferers should not take exercises. However, the exercises should be of a gentle nature like walking, gradually increasing the walk as the heart grows stronger. No strenuous exercise should be taken. As a general rule, the patient should take things quietly, avoiding excitement and physical strain. Plenty of rest, early hours for retiring, and lots of juices to build up the cells of the heart, are a MUST. The best juice combination is that of carrot combined with a little beet. At least two quarts daily should be taken, beginning with a pint and gradually increasing the amount consumed.

Wheat germ should be used each morning. This should be obtained fresh each week from a health food store and kept in a cold place. It may be taken with fruit juices or, after the whole wheat cereal is made for breakfast, a handful of wheat germ could be stirred in and served immediately. Vitamin E should also be taken in tablet form in severe cases of heart trouble, Alpha-Tocopherol being the kind which is generally recommended. It is best to get professional advice in connection with the use of Tocopherol.

"Fruit juices are apparently a good way to prevent coronary thrombosis, one of the worst of heart attacks," Dr. Ernest Klein reported in New

York Medicine published in May, 1949. Coronary thrombosis is the formation or the lodging of blood clots in the arteries leading to the heart. The clots block the arteries and part of the heart may die or be damaged from the lack of blood. The attacks come suddenly and often kill. "The fruit juice is combined with three-fourths water and a little sugar. It tends to make the human blood less thick and sticky, a thing that may cause the heart attack," he said. "Avoiding red meats and liver also helps."

The point to understand is that Nature provides everything to prevent any condition of ill-health and also to correct the condition once it has developed. All that is lacking is the intelligence to realize and accept nature's gifts.

Varicose Veins and Ulcers

Varicose veins are created, in the first place, by a toxic condition of the blood and also by poor circulation which may be caused by tight garters, or by pressure on the veins such as in pregnancy. Standing in one position for a long time also causes poor circulation in the legs—other similar conditions could also be mentioned. Due to their constant aching they make the sufferer irritable and, if left untreated may break and cause a serious ulcer. Much relief is obtained by bandaging the legs, especially with elastic bandages, as this affords some support and relieves the pressure, but the only permanent result is obtained by removing the causes.

The diet should be a natural one consisting chiefly of fruits, vegetables, whole grain products, with a little of the protein foods such as milk, eggs, nuts, cheese, fish or meat. There is usually a lack of Vitamin C, the vitamin which prevents fragility of the walls of the veins, so Vitamin C foods should be used abundantly.

Daily sun and air baths of the affected parts are very helpful, as is also the daily submerging of the legs for twenty minutes in cold water followed by a dry friction and hand massage, gently rubbing the legs upward, toward the heart. This stimulates the circulation of blood and tones up the veins.

While resting, day or night, the legs should be elevated by means of a cushion or raising the foot of the bed, so the veins are more relaxed.

In severe cases carrot poultices, of finely grated raw carrot between thin layers of cloth, may be applied. Another excellent compress is made of steeped calendula (marigold). The tops are steeped in water and cloths, wrung out of this decoction, applied to the ulcer. This could be kept on both day and night.

Where the veins appear large and clotted, but not broken, great relief has often been obtained by placing on them cold compresses of grapefruit skins finely grated.

Anything which tends to improve the circulation of the blood will be found very helpful in clearing up enlarged veins. Beet juice tends to improve both

the quality of the blood and also the circulation.
The beet juice should be taken in conjunction with
carrot or carrot and celery juice, or with tomato,
one-third beet juice being combined with two-
thirds of the milder juice.

CHAPTER 14

RESPIRATORY TROUBLES

Catarrhal Conditions

Vitamin A is necessary for the health of the skin, both inside and outside the body. If the inside skin is affected by this deficiency, the mucous membrane becomes weak, the excess mucous cannot be carried away and it may accumulate in different parts of the respiratory tract, causing a great deal of trouble and distress. This condition is called by various names, according to the location of these mucous deposits. Thus we have catarrh, sinus trouble, bronchitis, antrim trouble, asthma, bronchiectasis, or catarrhal deafness, all depending upon what part is affected. This mucous always settles in the weakest part of the body.

A person with any catarrhal condition should eat a great deal of raw yellow and green vegetables, as these are rich in Vitamin A. Carrot juice is one of the richest sources of Vitamin A and is in a form which the body can quickly utilize. Foods which are mucous-forming, such as cream, ice cream, whites of eggs, sugars and starches, should be cut to a minimum. To try to get rid of mucous without first stopping the intake of mucous-forming foods is about as senseless as trying to drain the sink without first turning off the tap.

The best way to get rid of the accumulation of mucous deposits in the system is through a fast as outlined under "General Directions." The fast should be broken as advised and then this diet should be followed as closely as possible:

BREAKFAST:—The best breakfast is that of fruit alone. This should be fresh, ripe, juicy fruits, no bananas, etc.

DINNER:—Mix together the following: 1 tbsp. honey, 2 tbsp. cream, 2 tbsp. raw oatmeal, juice of half a lemon, 2 raw grated apples, 2 tbsp. ground nuts, 2 tbsp. hot water. Serve fresh. As much of this mixture may be eaten as desired, but for best results, no other food of any kind should be taken during this meal. This is excellent for anyone, whether sick or well.

SUPPER—Several cooked vegetables, a little meat, egg yolks, cheese, nuts, or some meat substitute. (Do not use the whites of eggs). For dessert, either fresh or cooked fruit, sweetened with very little raw sugar or honey. A little skimmed milk may be had if desired, but very little cream.

Every morning, the sufferer should drink the juice of half a lemon diluted with water. This should be taken at least 20 minutes before breakfast if anything but fruit is had for that meal. In case of sinus trouble, a little lemon juice diluted in water could be sniffed far up the nostrils. For catarrhal deafness, take half a teaspoonful of horseradish grated and moistened with lemon juice. Hold this in the mouth a moment before swallowing it. This may bring tears to the eyes and make the nose run, but it is excellent in breaking up hardened mucous.

In May, 1949, Dr. C. Stewart Nash, in reporting to the New York State Medical Society, listed several medicinal products as producing deafness, one being quinine and another more recent medicine, streptomycin, which, he says, has been the cause of an alarmingly severe and possibly permanent inner ear damage.

Injections of Vitamin A have been given with good results in a great many cases of deafness—catarrhal deafness responding best of all to the treatment. This shows the close connection of Vitamin A to catarrhal conditions. Hence the diet should consist of quantities of raw juice from those vegetables which are yellow or green, in order to get a sufficient amount of the Vitamin A to correct the trouble.

Colds

From time immemorial, there have been numerous special "cures" for colds. People have an idea that they "catch" colds. This is far from the case, as the truth is that Man first produces the material in which the cold develops and places this material in the various parts of the body, including the nasal cavities. If this material was not placed there, he would never have a cold at all, just as mosquitoes could not breed without breeding places. This mucous deposit is made up of all the wastes from the excess of foods which are consumed—excesses which the body cannot use and cannot dispose of in a natural manner and hence are put away in convenient pockets in the body. Then any lowering of the body health level may cause inflammation in the mucous membrane, or this inflammation may be simply caused by this increasing deposit of waste matter. In any event, Nature attempts to unload this excess mucous, and this unloading is called a "cold."

When the cause is known, isn't it more sensible to help Nature to cleanse out this unwanted mucous, rather than try to suppress it? If it isn't cast from the body, it may do a great deal more harm than to cause a running nose, sniffles or a cough. And after all, a cough is merely one method that Nature has to bring the wastes from the chest area so it can be eliminated from the body by way of the mouth.

One of the latest "cures" for a cold is the Anti-Histamines which must be mentioned here to warn the unsuspecting public just what danger may lie ahead of them if they resort to drugs of this type. According to Quick magazine of January 2nd, 1950, these were the latest reports on the anti-histamine cold drugs: "1. The New York County Medical Society said anti-histamines tend to destroy white corpuscles in the blood. 2. A Johns Hopkins University professor said one person in five taking the pill will lose efficiency or appetite, get drowsy, suffer heart palpitation; 3. The Middlesex (N. J.) Medical Society called indiscriminate use of the drug "dangerous," reported one death from it; 4. Experts pointed out that the allergy theory of a cold, on which anti-histamine treatment is based, is not generally accepted."

Rather than trying to suppress the symptoms that are causing the distress, it is much better to try the following. At least it can do you no harm and is bound to make the entire body feel cleaner and, healthier.

The moment you feel the first symptoms of a cold, stop eating at once. Drink from 10 to 15 glasses of hot water a day, with lemon in every other glass, but no sugar. Take an enema every night, also a hot Epsom salts bath, using about two pounds of Epsom salts in the bath—no soap. Remain immersed in this bath for about 15 minutes then dry and go directly to bed, being careful to keep warm so as to induce perspiration. Instead of the hot water and lemon, faster results may be obtained by a combination of equal parts of onion juice, lemon juice, and honey, used in the porportion of one-fourth of this mixture to three-fourths boiling water. This combination may be made in advance, as it will keep indefinitely if capped and kept in the refrigerator.

Do not be alarmed if you are feverish. A fever is the result of Nature burning up excess wastes in the body and will soon abate if no more food or suppressive treatment is allowed. A cold towel placed on the forehead is found soothing. In Influenza, hot and cold compresses may be used over the area of the lungs. First use a towel wrung out of hot water—repeat this procedure two or three times—then apply one wrung out of cold water. This operation may be repeated several times daily.

The fast and above treatment should last from 3 to 7 days, according to the severity of the case.

During this time, no solid food of any kind should be taken, but after the first day, vegetable juices may be given freely—carrot and celery, or carrot, celery and beet juice is excellent, the beet juice being added if there is any fever. After the fever has abated, a diet of raw fruits and vegetables may be taken, then solid natural food, both raw and cooked, added later. If complete evacuations are not had daily, the enema should be used, for it is important that the bowels be kept clean. To ease the coughing, especially at night, take a teaspoonful of grated turnips with raw sugar or brown sugar. Honey is also good.

Colds, or indeed any of the catarrhal conditions, are caused by two things:—first, a lack in the diet of the necessary minerals and vitamins, to build up good healthy mucous membranes and, second, the over-eating of mucous forming foods. Therefore there is only one way to free one's self from colds, and that is by following a proper diet. If there is any tendency towards colds, one should be very careful to avoid the intake of those foods which are particularly mucous-forming.

Tuberculosis

This is definitely a disease brought on by a lack of calcium in the diet. The calcium intake, however, should be supplied with as little mucous as possible, as coughing to expel this mucous expends so much of the patient's energy. Hence, mucous-forming foods, such as milk (especially cream), ice cream, white of eggs, sugars and starches should be cut to a minimum. It is much better to find the supply of calcium in the vegetables and fruits, for here we find little mucous.

Rest, fresh air, and plenty of fruits and vegetables and their juices are necessary in the building and strengthening of the body, and this is especially true in the case of tuberculosis. A good juice combination is that of potato and carrot juice. After juicing potatoes, allow the starch to settle so the clear juice may be obtained. This should be mixed with carrot juice in equal proportions. Then to each glassful of this combination add 1 tbsp. of olive oil and the yolk of one egg (discarding the white, which is mucous forming). Beat till foamy before drinking. Several glasses should be taken daily.

Raw turnips, finely grated, and mixed with a little brown sugar is found very soothing to an irritated throat. When commencing to cough, it should be taken by the spoonful.

Foods which are high in calcium and which should therefore be included in the diet of anyone suffering from tuberculosis are: cheese, buttermilk, chard, watercress, cauliflower, broccoli, endive, celery, turnips, spinach, parsnips, carrots, oysters, molasses, raspberries, string beans, cabbage, oranges, rhubarb, lettuce, egg yolks, shrimp, lobsters, clams, almonds, dried beans, citrus fruits, bran, maple syrup.

Sunshine is excellent, but the lungs should be protected from the rays. Begin by exposing the feet for a few minutes each day, then the legs and thighs and abdomen, but protect the chest. Gradually increase the time of exposure so no burning will occur. If unable to take sun baths, a sun lamp may be used.

However, remember, in order to recover quickly, it is necessary to remove worry from the mind, for worry prevents or slows down Nature's power to heal.

CHAPTER 15

FOR LADIES ONLY

Female Troubles

The origin of female troubles of all kinds can usually be traced to three things: 1. Improper posture. 2. Improper clothing. 3. Improper diet.

So many women wear high heeled shoes which throw the whole body off balance; they wear tight fitting corsets which constrict the internal organs and put a downward pressure on the womb. This constriction also prevents the abdominal muscles from receiving the exercise they should have, and as a consequence, they grow slack. This tends to aggravate the downward trend of the internal organs.

Without proper diet the muscles cannot be built strong. If there is a lack of any of the necessary minerals or vitamins in the body, this lack will be reflected in the abdominal region as well as elsewhere. In this weakened congested area, aggravated by the constant pressure of the organs whose muscles are too weak to hold them in place, inflammation and serious trouble frequently develop.

Trouble may, of course, also be caused by uncleanliness, lack of proper care during childbirth, or the bearing of too many children. Then there are such causes as sex perversion, wilful abortion, certain methods of contraception or too much sexual indulgence. All this will cause malfunctioning of the female organs, and the only way to make them healthy again is to correct whatever is causing the trouble. Build up these organs through proper diet, proper care and proper posture, and there is little question about the results that will be achieved.

The diet should consist chiefly of fruits and vegetables and their juices, together with whole grain products, wheat germ or wheat germ oil, and a certain amount of protein foods such as meat, eggs, cheese, nuts, or fish.

The whole general health level of the body must be built up. This is best done through following the suggestions given under "General Rules." A long fast is not advised unless in serious cases, but a cleansing program should be instituted to begin with.

A bath should be taken each night and morning. Practice a few bending and stretching exercises each day—an especially good one is walking about the room on tip toe reaching upwards as fast as possible with the fingers as if trying to touch the stars. Do this while in the bare feet. Exercises should preferably be taken in the morning.

Each morning sit in warm water for a while, then let the cold water run into the tub, increasing the coldness gradually until the water is as cold as can be borne. Dash the cold water onto the pelvic region, then dry quickly with a rough towel until the skin glows. This tones up the muscles of the abdomen.

A good juice combination for female trouble is equal parts of carrot and celery juice with a small amount of parsley and spinach juice added. Do not use too much of the two latter juices, as it may prove nauseating. Always make the drink palatable by adding enough carrot juice. About two quarts daily should be taken. Instead of parsley and spinach juice, beet juice should be substituted frequently.

In severe cases, a wine glassful of clear beet juice may be taken twice daily, besides drinking the above combination.

If overweight, follow the diet suggested in the chapter in this subject, as too much fat causes more pressure and, hence, more congestion in this region.

Do not wear any tight fitting garments and, through exercises, built up the abdominal muscles till such time as no corsets will be required. Change to shoes with lower heels. This will probably have to be done gradually, as the use of high heels tend to shorten the muscles in the calves of the legs and the sudden transition from high to low heels will cause great distress. Use heels slightly lower and, when the legs become accustomed to them, then heels still lower, till sensible heels can be worn without distress.

In prolapsus, or falling of the womb, there must be exercise to build up the muscles which, ordinarily, would hold these organs in place. Of course, any tendency towards tight clothing or any heavy lifting, stooping, etc., must be avoided at first till the muscles are strengthened.

It is best to go for a few days on a juice diet to lighten the load in the intestinal tract. Enemas should be taken each night. Follow this with a natural diet as suggested above, eating light meals and drinking about two quarts of raw juices daily. This is to clear the colon of accumulations of putrid matter which may cause gas and pressure.

The hot Epsom salts baths should be taken several times weekly, also every morning the dry friction bath, rubbing the entire body thoroughly each morning with a rough towel till the skin glows, to promote better circulation.

The Sitz-bath is also found to be very valuable in this connection. It is taken as follows: place two large dish pans, small tubs, or baby baths, side by side. Put 4 or 5 inches of hot water in one and the same amount of cold water in the other. Sit in the hot bath for about five minutes, then one minute in the cold. Repeat 3 or 4 times. This may be done every day till the condition is corrected. Or hot and cold water may be run alternately into the bath tub.

It is very important that each day for a certain period of time, the body be relaxed, with the feet in a position about 18 inches higher than the head. This can be accomplished by raising the foot of the bed or, better still, by lying on a prolapsus board. Long ago, if an Indian woman had prolapsed organs, she would lay over the side of a hill with her feet tied to a stake. This relaxing should be carried on for about an hour each day and, in severe cases, several times daily.

A good exercise to strengthen the abdominal muscles and to bring the organs back into position is that of lying flat on the floor and raising the feet and legs to a position above the head. If possible, continue this exercise till you can touch the floor above the head with the toes.

The stomach and intestines are held in place by certain muscles which grow weak when they are not used. If these muscles lose their strength or "tone" the result may be constipation, and sagging of the stomach and intestines. It is estimated that 90 percent of men and women develop this sagging condition after the age of forty. In some this condition has not developed to the danger point and there may be only vague symptoms of discomfort.

The reasons for this sagging condition should be corrected at once. There should be proper nutrition to build strong muscle cells, there should be proper posture to allow the organs to remain in their proper places. Remember, if muscles are not used they tend to weaken; if they are used they will grow strong.

The same corrective measures apply to prolapsed stomach and intestines as to prolapsed female organs. Every home should have a prolapsus board on which to lie and relax. This is the easiest and quickest way to assist nature in returning the organs to their proper position than anything that has yet been devised. Of course, only by strengthening the muscles will these organs remain in their correct positions.

After a few days of just relaxing on this board, certain exercises should be undertaken. By placing a sandbag on the abdomen, the muscles will be strengthened. This may be carried out as follows: Lie on the prolapsus board, which will immediately bring the organs back to their correct positions, then place the sandbag low on the pelvic area. Draw in the abdomen as far as possible, pressing the bag down firmly, holding this position for about 15 seconds. Then relax. Then push the abdomen, with the sandbag still resting on it, out as far as possible, holding it for about the same length of time. Repeat this exercise—in—out—in—out, etc. Begin with short periods and gradually increase them each day as the abdominal muscles grow stronger.

Pre-Natal Care

A research was made a few years ago in the maternity division of the Toronto General Hospital as to the effect of diet on the course of pregnancy and the health of expectant mothers and newborn infants. Women, who were to have their babies about the same time, were divided into two groups—the one group being placed on a proper diet. The other group remained on their accustomed meals.

As reported in the Toronto Daily Star:

"It was discovered that the mothers who, during their pregnancy, ate balanced meals, including vitamin concentrates, had a safe delivery and that both they and their babies were in much better health than the mothers who, during the same period were on poor diets. The latter developed complications during pregnancy, and at the birth they had a much harder time than did the mothers who had a proper diet. Eleven mothers in the poor diet group lost their babies through such complications as prematurity, still birth, convulsions, etc., whereas only two mothers in the good diet group had such complications. Among the mothers on the poor diets, there were several deaths and serious illnesses, but none among those whose diets were good."

Dr. Ebbs summed up in his official report: "There were fewer infections, less fever, less anemia and, all in all, less complications which worried the obstetrical staff, among patients whose diets were good. By improving deficient prenatal diet, the whole course of pregnancy can be improved and the condition of the child also."

It was reported at the time that the doctors could go through the nursery and, without mistake, pick out the babies from the good diet group.

It might be added in this connection that raw vegetable juices are the best vitamin concentrates, as the natural foods contain many vitamins that have not yet been discovered, and the minerals and vitamins are contained in groups, not found singly.

The diet should consist of plenty of fruits and

vegetables and their juices, and be very low in starches and sugars. The weight of the baby should not exceed 7 lbs. as there is plenty of time to add fat after the child is delivered—if fat is desired. The unborn child will need plenty of the organic minerals, and these should be supplied in the natural foods. The diet should consist of whole grain breads, vegetables, fruits, and proteins such as meat, eggs, cheese, milk, cottage cheese, nuts or fish. If unable to take sun baths, Vitamin D should be taken in capsule form. Fresh wheat germ should be taken every day to supply the Vitamin E required. The meat intake should be limited. When the mother's diet is deficient in organic minerals, the minerals in her own body will be taken to form the new life, thus she may expect to find decayed teeth if she does not consume enough calcium foods. This, we can see, but we cannot see the other minerals being stolen from more vital parts of her body. This is going on, nevertheless, and the mother will surely suffer if her diet is not correct.

A daily warm bath should be taken in the evening and, in the morning a dry friction rub with a rough towel to promote circulation. Deep breathing exercise and walking are very valuable up to a month before the baby is expected. The housework should be attended to as usual, but as much time as possible should be spent out of doors. Avoid stooping or stretching or lifting anything heavy. The following exercises are especially advised, and should be performed about ten times each, if possible, without growing tired:

1. Lie on your back with arms outstretched, draw up the knees to the chest, and clasping the arms

around them, attempt to touch the head to the knees; resume starting position.

2. On hands and knees, push the head and body as far forward as possible, then back as far as possible. Repeat ten times. This keeps the spinal column limber.

3. Lying on the back, place the hands under the hips, then raise first one leg, then the other. Repeat ten times.

When beginning these exercises, start with only a few, stopping before becoming tired, gradually increasing as the muscles are strengthened. These exercises are designed to strengthen muscles and keep them supple so there will be no chance of a hard birth.

If the patient is subject to morning sickness, get out of the house as soon as possible after breakfast. Walk at least two miles a day, easing up towards the ninth month. The sucking of a lemon will often relieve this feeling of nausea.

Besides taking carrot and celery juice, add watercress juice if this is available. Also kelp tablets should be taken to ensure the supply of iodine. This may be obtained from any good health food store.

All undue strain, worry or excitement is to be avoided. Give your child a proper start in life, and this "start" begins when the child is conceived.

CHAPTER 16

NERVES

C. W. Beers has made the statement that, in the state of New York, one person out of every 22 has to be placed in an asylum at one time or another. The feeble-minded or mentally ill outnumber the consumptives in the United States by eight to one, and these statistics show only those treated in general hospitals. Besides this number there are those taken care of in private hospitals and those who are not treated at all.

Disease of the mind is just as real a disease as are cases of heart trouble and, therefore, should be treated as such by building up the entire health level. When the health is good there is less tendency to worry, which is usually the first symptom of a mind that is not adjusted to the environment of the individual. Dr. Alexis Carroll stated, "Dementia Praecox and circular insanity manifest themselves more especially where life is restless and disordered, food too elaborate or too poor and syphilis frequent, and also when the nervous system is hereditarily unstable, when moral discipline has been suppressed, when selfishness, irresponsibility, and dispersion are customary."

The first thing of importance is to change the diet to one containing all the necessary minerals and vitamins. The next is to change the way of living. Stop working so hard. Take life a little easier. Get a hobby. This hobby should be some-

thing in which the patient is interested—some
different from the regular work being perform
If a mental worker, then the hobby should be one
in which the large muscles are used. As Dale
Carnegie says, "You can't think of two things at
the same time." So, if you are working at something you are not apt to be worrying about
something else. And, remember, you don't have to
carry the whole load by yourself. It is easy for
someone to say, "Don't worry," but this is easier
to say than do. If you feel that you are alone, it
helps a great deal. Memorize this verse:

> "The World is wide
> In Time and Tide
> And God is Guide
> So do not hurry.
> The man is blest
> Who does his best
> And leaves the rest.
> So do not worry." — G. J. Termansen

Say it to yourself several times daily, especially
when you start to worry. It will do wonders to give
you a sense of peace and protection.

Live one day at a time. Do not worry about the
future or waste regrets on the past. Try to make
each day as perfect as possible and the next day
will take care of itself.

"Look to this day, for it is Life, the very life of
life. In its brief course lie all the verities and
realities of our existence; the bliss of growth, the
splendor of beauty, the glory of action. For yesterday is but a dream, and tomorrow is only a vision,

but each day well lived makes every yesterday a dream of happiness and every tomorrow a vision of hope. Look well therefore, unto this day."—Sanskript.

No one can go out under the stars and ponder the thought that those millions of heavenly bodies are swirling onwards out there in space, each in its own orbit, and each following a law, without realizing that there must be some Supreme Intelligence at work. Or watch the living things on this earth—how everything follows the directions of this Natural Law of Supreme Intelligence. Plant a seed and, even if that seed is upside down, the roots will always grow down into the earth and the stem will grow upwards. And, if that root approaches some poisonous metal bar, it will veer off and go around that metal rather than touch it, for something within the plant knows that to touch it is to die. Surely no one can doubt that there is an Innate Intelligence, a spark of the Supreme Intelligence, within each living thing, that directs its actions.

Some people will not allow themselves to believe in anything they cannot prove with their senses. Yet who knows what electricity is? Who can prove what causes it? Nevertheless, by following certain laws, we can make use of its power. If we break these laws, we are in danger.

Puny man, with his "ignorant knowledge" puts himself out of harmony with the natural laws and finds himself in difficulties—difficulties which he finds impossible to solve till he puts himself back in harmony with those laws so the Innate can work for him and direct him. There is so much that man cannot understand and probably never will understand, but this Innate will direct him if he will only allow it to do so.

One of the most beautiful New Year's messages ever delivered was that broadcast several years ago by King George to the people of the British Empire:

"And I said to the man at the gate of the year, 'Give me a light that I may tread safely into the unknown.'

'Go out into the darkness and put your hand into the hand of God. That shall be better than light and safer than the known way'."

The emotions affect all the various parts of the body. When a person becomes angry, his face becomes either flushed or pale, and his muscles may become so tense that he begins to tremble. If this emotion arises when he is eating he may lose all appetite or perhaps develop a bad case of indigestion. Negative emotions such as fear, jealousy, anger, worry, hatred, etc., all have serious effects on the system, especially if repeated often. It shows poor adjustment to life's problems, but it is much easier to give advice on this subject than to correct one's reactions to problems. One should put into practice one of Goethe's adages, "Every day's duty is to be happy."

Perhaps the best way to correct the habit of worrying is to analyse oneself. One worries only about what one fears is going to happen. Remember, the worst never happens. Write down exactly what it is that you are afraid of. Get all the data you can on the subject and try to do something constructive about it. If necessary, consult someone who is capable of giving expert advice. The cure for anything is only accomplished by removing the cause.

Change the color scheme of your rooms, or, if this is not feasible, at least get some colored sheets or something cheerful to look at. Get out of doors as much as possible for leisurely walks in the fresh air and sunshine. And breathe deeply. A deep breather is never nervous. Rest whenever tired. Worry causes tenseness and tenseness causes disease as it shuts off circulation. Whenever you find a negative thought coming into your mind, think immediately about something pleasant. You cannot think of two things at the same time, so substitute positive thoughts such as love, courage, happiness, unselfishness and confidence. It has been well said that "Thoughts are things." They can make you well or ill, and only you can control them. You attract unto yourself that which your mind thinks about. If you think health and joy and good fortune, they shall be your lot, but if you think selfishness or hatred or disappointment, they shall come to you just as surely.

A quotation which has helped a great many people for years and which should become a general maxim and put into practice by everyone, is this:

"If you don't feel the way you ought to act, then act the way you ought to feel, and you'll feel the way you ought to act."

You will be surprised how this works. Try it.

A person suffering from nerve trouble of any kind should have a lot of food containing Sodium and Vitamin B. All green, leafy foods contain an abundance of these elements—lettuce and celery being especially valuable. The green celery and the green leaves of the lettuce should be used, as there is not as much value in the head lettuce, or in bleached celery.

It is more advisable for the nervous person to eat vegetable salads and properly cooked vegetables than to have much fresh fruit. Fruit is a cleanser and may irritate the nerves. So until the body is in a less toxic condition, every other day will be found often enough to have fresh fruit. The diet should be an alkaline one, eliminating as far as possible such acid-forming foods as starches, sugars and fried foods. Any sweetening should be of the natural kind, such as raw sugar, molasses, brown sugar or honey. Any starches should be of the whole grain variety, such as a whole wheat or rye breads or cereals, and bread should never be fresh. Any whole grain used as a cereal should be cooked thin and then, when it is done, add a handful of wheat germ and serve immediately. Tea, coffee and alcoholic drinks should be eliminated entirely from the diet.

There should be a great deal of rest, 10 hours not

being too much for a person with bad nerves. One simple thing that has proved to be very effective in a great many cases is to take a leisurely hot bath at night, drink a glass of celery juice, and go directly to bed. Relax completely for twenty minutes, not attempting to sleep but merely to relax all over.

In the morning rub your entire body briskly with a rough towel to promote better circulation.

Take at least two quarts of vegetable juices daily, the combination found most helpful being carrot and celery or carrot and lettuce. Always make the drink palatable by adding enough carrot juice.

If troubled with insomnia, do not eat before going to bed. Food produces energy, and the habit of taking a snack before retiring has caused many a sleepless night. The celery juice will help relax the nerves and satisfy any craving for nourishment.

The habit of placing the feet in a bath of hot water for about 15 minutes before retiring is also a great help and could be used whenever the full bath is not taken. This draws about 50% of the blood from the congested brain and allows one to relax better. After retiring some people have been able to go to sleep merely by reading a very uninteresting book. Even if they woke in the night and felt they couldn't go back to sleep, if they started to read this type of book they would fall asleep immediately. Their minds would go to sleep rather than be forced to concentrate on such an uninteresting subject.

One lady and her husband, who had been greatly troubled with insomnia, found that the celery juice at night was all that they required to obtain a peaceful sleep. She writes, "Both my husband and myself have found celery juice to be a nerve tonic. Whereas from a nerve-tasking day of work, sleep seemed to run away, now from a glass of celery juice we are afforded a peaceful night of refreshing sleep."

Epilepsy

Begin with a fast from four to five days as outlined under "General Directions." During this time, plenty of celery and carrot juice should be taken. Break the fast as directed. The following diet should be adopted for from 7 to 14 days:—

MORNING: Celery and carrot juice.

MIDDAY MEAL: Raw salad, composed of any of the vegetables in season attractively prepared. Dressing, if any is used, should consist of olive oil and lemon juice. Dessert: raisins or soaked prunes, figs or dates.

EVENING MEAL: Raw salad, one or two cooked vegetables such as spinach, cabbage, carrots, turnips, cauliflower, etc. Finish the meal with a few nuts.

If bread or potatoes or other starchy food is taken, the effect of the diet will be lost. Nothing should be added to the above list if good results are desired. No drinks other than water and the juice of fruits or vegetables should be taken. With regard to quantity, let hunger be your guide. After this diet is discontinued, an alkaline diet should be followed. Meat should not be used, while bread, sugar, rich cake, pastries, puddings, pies, and all starch food should be studiously avoided. No tea, coffee, or intoxicating drinks, or cocoa, should be used, and no seasoning or spices. The diet should be as light as possible. Fresh raw vegetables, Nature's healing foods, should form the major part of the diet, supplemented with a little whole grain cereal with wheat germ added after the cereal is cooked, and a little cereal with wheat germ added after the cereal is cooked, and a little cheese, cottage cheese or nuts.

A daily bath should be taken and simple exercises to tone up the system. An Epsom salts bath consisting of 1 lb. of Epsom salts to the bath of hot water—no soap—should be taken twice weekly. Remain immersed for from 15 to 20 minutes, massaging every part of the body. Then dry and go directly to bed. Another very useful thing is the application of alternate hot and cold compresses to the base of the brain, at the back of the neck where the head joins the neck. The patient sits with his feet in a bowl of hot water, and first a towel wrung out of hot water and next a towel wrung out of cold water is applied to this area. This should be repeated several times. When the case is severe, it may be repeated several times daily. The number of hot and cold applications may be anywhere from 2 of each to 4 or 5 of each, depending upon the severity of the case.

Spinal manipulation has also, in many cases, proved valuable.

The fasts and restricted period of the diet should be repeated at 2 or 3 months intervals.

JUICES ADVISED: Celery juice is the best juice for the nerves. To make it more palatable, carrot juice should be added, about half and half. Lettuce juice is also excellent.

Effect of Vitamin B₁ on Health

The following is a quotation from the Yearbook of Agriculture, published by the United States Department of Agriculture:

"Although a complete lack of Vitamin B1 in the human dietary may result in the occurrence of beriberi, there may be many degrees of the deficiency causing less well defined symptoms. Any degree, from the mild form in which slight and unrecognizable symptoms occur, to the extreme case with severe metabolic disturbances, may occur in persons of all ages.

"In the early stages the adult may complain of fatigue, stiffness, headache, nervousness, and loss of appetite. Later any one of these three types may be recognized:

(1) "The so-called wet, beriberi type (called wet because of the appearance of large amounts of fluid in the tissues, causing a general edema), regarded by some investi-

gators as a critical stage in the development of the disease, in which swelling of the tissues is probably caused by improper functioning of the heart;

(2) "The dry beriberi type, considered to be a chronic form which may exist over a long period with possible involvement of nervous system changes; and

(3) "A type in which enlargement of the heart and related conditions may be found. The occurrence of (2) is a condition in which control of the muscles is affected, causing a loss of coordination in the movements particularly of the feet, legs and arms. In severe cases even the muscles of the trunk may be affected. Patients in such advanced stages of the disease develop ataxia—uncontrolled muscle contractions—and lack of coordination.

"This deficiency disease is of course prevented by the use of well-balanced diets . . . A well-balanced diet is a further essential of the curative procedure. It seems clear that although the primary deficiency in beriberi is Vitamin B1 there may be a lack of other nutritional factors as well, factors that can most successfully be supplied by proper dietary means. This is true in the case of other dietary deficiencies also, but particularly true of Vitamin B1, because an early symptom of the disease, loss of appetite, results in reduced food intake, and, in turn, a reduced supply of other essential substances.

"It (Vitamin B1) is destroyed by heat in the presence of moisture."

It will be seen from this last statement that the vitamin is destroyed by cooking the vegetables, so it must be obtained from the RAW vegetables.

The human body is unable to store amounts of Vitamin B1, therefore it is important to maintain a constant supply in the diet.

CHAPTER 17

UNDERWEIGHT

A calorie is the amount of food material needed to raise the body temperature one degree. If more energy is expended, more heat is produced and so more calories are burned up. If more calories are taken into the system than are burned up or eliminated, the result is that they are stored in the body in the form of fat. There are about 4000 calories in a pound of fat, so the more calories absorbed the quicker will one gain weight.

It is important that the underweight person learns to relax, for most underweights are nervous and highstrung, and, wherever there is tenseness, there is also poor circulation, and where there is poor circulation in the digestive tract, the food is not properly assimilated. A few thin people have an enormous appetite and yet they seem to stay as thin as ever no matter how much food they consume. It is simply that they do not relax and let the food be digested. They will often say, after being joshed about the amount of food they eat, "It keeps me thin carrying it around." No wonder they eat so much—they are actually starving to death no matter how much they consume, for they cannot assimilate the value of what they are eating.

It often happens, too, that there is a great deal of mucous lining the intestines, and this prevents the absorption of the digested food. You are not so much a product of what you eat as you are of what you assimilate.

However, the majority of thin people are not, as a rule, big eaters, nor do they eat the foods which put on weight. Notice the people in the restaurants who order double malteds or the ice cream sundaes dripping with chocolate syrup, and you will generally find that those orders go to people who are already very much overweight. Thin people, as a rule, have very little appetite. Vitamin B Complex stimulates the appetite, and so is of great value in cases of underweight. And as it is usually hard for them to assimilate the value of the raw vegetables, these should be taken in liquid form. Did you notice that when a person takes a glass of liquor, it does not matter whether he is thin or fat, whether he has good or poor powers of assimilation, he still feels the effect of that drink within a few minutes. This is also true of raw vegetable juices. The Vitamin B Complex is found in most vegetables, but the following are rich sources: carrots, cabbage, spinach, watercress, turnip leaves, parsley, dandelion, as well as cocoanut. The diet should consist chiefly of:

JUICES: Carrot juice, carrot juice and cream, carrot juice and celery juice. Also any of the above mentioned vegetables can be used in the form of juice.

GRAINS: Any cooked whole grain cereals served with brown sugar and cream, with added wheat germ, whole grain bread and muffins served with butter.

SOUPS: Any cream soups.

VEGETABLES: Starchy vegetables contain more calories than the green leafy ones, so it is wise to take the latter in the form of juice and eat the starchy ones such as beans, corn, potatoes (escalloped or cooked in other forms and served with butter), yams and succotash.

PROTEINS: Cream cheese or American cheese, eggs, salmon or other fatty fish, stew, mutton chop or roast mutton, roast duck, roast goose, cocoanuts, filberts, hickory nuts, pecans, walnuts.

FRUITS: Ripe bananas, figs, dates, baked apple served with cream and honey, raisins, and prunes stewed and sweetened.

DESSERTS: All desserts served with or containing cream.

SALADS: All salads should be served with cream cheese or salad dressing.

In general, the amount of proteins should be decreased and the amount of natural sugars and starches and fats increased. However, this might be a dangerous procedure if one did not consume the raw vegetable juices. These contain the necessary minerals and vitamins to protect the body against cell deterioration.

Nature is always trying to normalize the system. If one only cleans out the debris and gives nature the material to work with, one need not fear the outcome.

Keep the intestines clean. Take a certain amount of exercise daily—the best exercise being a leisurely walk, breathing deeply and thinking of pleasant subjects. Get plenty of rest and sleep. Keep the mind calm.

If at all anemic, the yolk of an egg could be added to a glass of carrot juice and taken several times daily. Also cocoanut powder can be added to the carrot juice. It not only adds a delicious flavor, but it also contains a great many calories.

CHAPTER 18

OVERWEIGHT—"THE BATTLE OF THE BULGE"

To understand the danger of overweight, one has but to read life insurance statistics. An overweight person is a poor risk; the greater the risk the less desire the insurance company has to take the policy. But, aside from the fact that the overweight condition may shorten life by many years, no one wants to carry this excess baggage, if merely for the sake of appearance. No one likes to buy clothes designed to hide the bulges—they feel ashamed every time they try on a new suit or dress.

There have been volumes written on this subject and numerous reducing drugs put on the market, but the only safe way to reduce is to take into the body less calories than the body requires and to see that this diet supplies all the necessary minerals and vitamins that are needed by the cells. The amount of calories vary with the individual and with the type of work which he does. Food is a fuel, and this fuel is converted by the body into energy in the same way that a steam engine converts coal into energy to run the train. Some people have wonderful powers of digestion and absorption and yet burn up the fuel very slowly, while others do not absorb as much from their food and yet burn faster what they do absorb, and so they remain thin. It is like two furnaces, one with the draft open and the other with the draft partly closed. As the diet approaches more nearly a natural one, the better are the drafts adjusted so the food is burned at a more normal rate. The harder the work done, the more fuel is required and so the greater amount of calories needed by the body. Housewives or sedentary workers use up about 2400 calories, but this, of course, varies with the individual. If, therefore, they eat less than this amount Nature draws on the store of fat in the body and commences to burn that fuel. A reduction diet should consist of from 1200 to 1500 calories per day. This would mean a loss of about a pound and a half a week. If exercises are taken, more fuel is required and so more of the stored fat will be burned up, which would result in a faster loss in weight. But the chief value of exercise is to keep the body from becoming "flabby."

The average reducing diet is actually dangerous, as it does not provide the body with the minerals and vitamins required for healthy cells and, as a result, a person becomes irritable and makes life miserable both for himself and everyone he comes in contact with, and so is often persuaded to give up the diet. However, the addition of raw vegetable juices to a reducing diet makes it easy to reduce with safety. So this should be a reducer's slogan, "Reduce with Juice."

A program which has helped a great many back to a normal figure is: Follow the suggestions as outlined under "General Directions," beginning with a fast of from four to five days, then break the fast as advised, on a large raw salad. Then this diet could be used:

BREAKFAST: Fruit salad and a glass of vegetable juice.

LUNCHEON: Large glass of vegetable juice; one boiled egg; one large green salad.

EVENING MEAL: One sliced ripe tomato, two steamed non-starchy vegetables, such as string beans, turnips, cabbage, carrots, parsnips, with a very little butter; two slices broiled liver or other lean meat, a serving of fruit salad.

These are sample meals and are well balanced, as they include plenty of bulk as well as the necessary minerals and vitamins to build up the general strength, while most acid-forming and fat-forming foods are excluded. Three things in particular must be cut to a minimum: FAT, SUGAR and STARCH. All cooked vegetables should be either baked or steamed—otherwise valuable minerals and vitamins will be destroyed. Fruit and vegetable juices should be taken whenever desired. In fact, they are essential in any diet, for without them there is almost certain to be a vitamin or mineral deficiency, and the desired results are not obtained.

It has been found that if persons on a reducing diet become hungry they should have strips of raw carrots or pieces of raw cabbage to nibble on, as this gives them something for the digestive juices to act upon and thus the sensation of hunger disappears. The digestion of raw vegetables burns up more energy than is obtained from them, so are actually slimming foods. It is only when the digestive juices are poured into the stomach and there is nothing to dilute them, or for them to act upon, that this sensation of hunger occurs. Vegetables and fruits are easily digested and quickly leave the stomach, and so the sensation of hunger occurs more frequently upon a diet of fruits and vegetables than upon a diet of meats or other protein food. It has been found by many that if they eat oftener, they reduce without distress. There is nothing fattening in the raw vegetables, so these may be taken in abundance whenever desired. The vegetable juices, too, have often been found to disperse the feeling of hunger.

It is also necessary to keep interested in something, otherwise a person is more prone to think of their sensations and will often imagine that they are hungry when they just lack something more interesting to do than eating.

Exercises should be taken each morning. Walking is one of the best exercises. Every morning, wash the face and neck in warm water, and then splash cold water over them, as this tightens skin which was previously stretched with the underlying excess fat. This prevents the sagging skin noticed by some who are on a reducing diet. In fact, the whole body would be better for this treatment. Or wash the whole body with warm water, then rub it briskly with a towel dipped in cold water.

Vegetable juices, containing carrot and celery (or swiss chard) and a little cabbage juice is excellent. Lemon juice in plain water—no sugar—is also an excellent thing to take, as it quenches thirst. There should be as little salt as possible in the diet, as salt holds particles of water in the system and causes puffiness.

CHAPTER 19

EYE TROUBLE

During the war, raw carrots and carrot juice were used extensively by the Army, the Navy, and the Air Force, especially where good eyesight was of vital importance. Carrot juice contains a great deal of Vitamin A, which people have come to associate with eyesight. Durling, the columnist, wrote in his column in the Seattle Post-Intelligencer, "A Berkeley, Calif., subscriber says that three eye specialists told him his eyesight was failing so rapidly he would be blind in two years. All the specialists said nothing could be done about it. Then a friend suggested to this man that he try drinking carrot juice. He did. As a result, he says, his eye condition is completely cured. Not only that, the carrot juice habit seems to have made his hair grow. At any rate, he has much more hair than when he started to consume carrot juice regularly."

The eyes are merely the indication of the health level of the entire body and trouble in any part of that body can show up in defective eyesight. Thus the eyes can be affected if one has liver trouble, kidney trouble, diabetes, or any other disease of the various organs. Hence, it is just as important, in defective vision, to go on a program of good cleansing and rebuilding as it is in any other diseased condition. The body should have a good cleansing through fasting and purging, even if for only one day a week, till results are obtained. For a week, if possible, nothing should be taken except distilled water, fruit and vegetable juices but, if very hungry, oranges or grapefruit may be eaten. Follow the suggestions under "General Rules." Results may be obtained without the fast, but will possibly be slower.

Then gradually add to the above cooked vegetables and raw salads, including an abundance of the yellow and green foods, as they are rich in Vitamin A—the vitamin so greatly needed in the correction of poor eyesight. Do not use strong tea, coffee, or cocoa, or any alcoholic beverages.

It is important that the bowels be kept open so, for the time being, if constipated, follow the direction in the chapter on "Elimination."

Several times daily for 15-minute periods, try reading without glasses, blinking the eyes frequently, especially at the end of the lines. Then try to lengthen the period of reading without glasses. Try to do without your glasses as much as possible without causing eyestrain. If near-sighted, try to coax the eyes to see farther by gradually increasing the distance of reading. If far-sighted, gradually bring the paper closer to the eyes, thus coaxing the eyes to focus properly. Remember, the mind is master of the actions of the body.

For 15-minute periods, about three times daily, close the eyes, resting the elbows on the knees and, putting the palms over the eyes, with the fingers crossed, think of looking into velvety blackness and completely relax. This helps to relax the muscles of the eyes and the nerves controlling the sight, and this alone often works wonders, as a great deal of eye trouble is caused by tension.

Dr. William Councilman Owen and Ella Uhler Owens of Johns Hopkins University Medical School, Baltimore, told the American Public Health Association in New York that Vitamin E is showing promise of checking a disease causing blindness in premature infants. This addition of Vitamin E has been administered the first week after birth with very encouraging results. Hence, everyone should see that they get wheat germ daily.

At the State University of Iowa some time ago, Dr. C. D. O'Brien and his co-workers, experimenting with animals, were able to produce cataracts of the eye when the diet lacked Vitamin G.

In research work conducted by the Department of Swine Husbandry, University of Texas, it was discovered that pigs, fed continuiously on a diet devoid of Vitamin A, had offspring born with no eyes whatsoever. This proved the absolute necessity of this vitamin in the formation of the eye cells. These eyeless pigs were then fed on a diet rich in Vitamin A, and all their offspring had normal eyesight. This is what is known in science as the reversible demonstration.

Dr. David O. Harrington in the American Journal of Ophthalmology states that many disturbances and diseases of the eye are wholly or partly "psychogenic" (caused by the mind), and greater attention should be paid to emotional problems in seeking to cure them. Glaucoma, which may lead to total blindness, is due to defective circulation in the vessels which supply blood to the eyes, and since circulation is controlled by the central nervous system, emotional conflict may affect it. Hence, it is of utmost importance to first feed the body the materials which are needed to build good healthy eye cells, and next to learn to relax and help your mind direct the flow of the blood to all affected parts of the body. As long as there is tension and strain, the flow of blood to the various organs is impeded.

The following quotation from the Yearbook of Agriculture clearly illustrates the importance of Vitamin A in the diet.

"Animals fed on rations very low in Vitamin A value show evidence of several successive stages of deficiency, increasing in severity until death ensues. Practically all of these stages of Vitamin A deficiency have at one time or another been observed in human beings, also.

"The earliest recognizable sign of such a deficiency is night blindness, a visual abnormality that makes the eyes less responsive to dim illumination. After being exposed to a bright light, the eyes of a night-blind person cannot adjust in the darkness to the same low degree of illumination as can the eyes of well-nourished persons. Common examples of the difficulty a night-blind person has in seeing in a dim light include his problem of visual adjustment when he enters a dimly lighted theater from a brightly illuminated entrance or when driving an automobile he tries to see the dark road after a car with bright headlights has passed.

"Night-blindness due to Vitamin A deficiency can be quickly relieved by increasing the intake of foods rich in Vitamin A. Yellow and leafy green vegetables are rich in carotenes. (The body uses the carotenes to manufacture Vitamin A).

"A more severe or a more prolonged Vitamin A deficiency results in extreme muscular weakness and changes in the structure of certain body cells which form the protective covering of every surface of the body, including the surface of the ducts and cavities within the body. The changes in these cell structures interfere with their proper functioning.

"Late stages of such deficiency are accompanied by a serious type of eye disease which if it progresses leads to permanent blindness."

Stop day-dreaming. Try to notice the things about you more, and try to train your memory to recall what you have seen. Look around for a moment, then close your eyes and see how many things you can recall having looked at. Lie in the sun occasionally with the eyelids closed. Begin with short periods of two or three minutes and gradually increase the period each day, being careful, of course, not to become sunburned.

Remember, a lack of Vitamin A in the diet

weakens the eyesight and can cause various eye ailments. Carrot juice is a rich source of this vitamin and can be taken in abundance. When available, parsley juice should be added to the carrot juice. About 2 quarts daily may be taken.

CHAPTER 20

CHILDREN'S DISEASES

Polio

The minds of many parents are filled with dread of Polio. A great deal of money has been collected to try to find some miracle drug which will cure helpless victims of this disease, but very little is done along research in dietetics to try to find out the cause and prevention of this crippler. A few outstanding doctors are proving the relation of this disease to a deficiency diet, but very little attention is paid to it. The following are articles which appeared recently in newspapers:

"Pasadena, Calif.—Lack of Vitamin C makes fatigued persons easy prey for infantile paralysis, according to Dr. Joseph C. Risser, bone specialist and president-elect of the American Academy of Applied Nutrition. Loss of Vitamin C or lack of it in one's diet is dangerous, he declares, to bone health because the vitamin supplies caliogen, the intercellular material which deposits calcium in the bones."

"Science Editor William S. Barton in Los Angeles Times, reports that Dr. Fred R. Klenner stated that all the 60 polio patients treated, during the 1948 epidemic at Reidsville, N.C., with 100 to 200 mg. of Vitamin C, were well after 72 hours. The dosage varied according to the age of the sufferer. This vitamin was injected between the veins or muscles and the dose was repeated again two hours later if no immediate drop in temperature resulted. And again, two hours later, continuing in this manner for 24 hours unless temperature dropped in the meantime. After the temperature dropped, it was given in the same manner every six hours for the next 48 hours. A few relapses occurred, but after resumption of the treatment for another 48 hours, the relapsed patients recovered."

Ten years ago Dr. Claus Jungeblut, Columbia University bacteriologist, found, in an experiment with monkeys, that six times as many monkeys were saved if Vitamin C was used as when it was not used. Also they had more resistance to polio when the diet had been high in Vitamin C before they were injected with the polio organism.

In a Yearbook of the U. S. Department of Agriculture, titled, "Food and Life," we find this statement: "In Vitamin C deficiency the cells which produce intercellular substances undergo striking changes. The nutrition and structure of the teeth are affected very early in the absence of Vitamin C intake. Later the tiny capillary blood vessels become weakened and cause hemorrhages throughout the body, the joints become swollen, and the bones become porous and fragile. These symptoms are characteristic of the Vitamin C deficiency diseases."

Surely, with this knowledge available, more publicity should be given to the fact that polio is definitely linked up with a nutritional lack. Every mother should make it her responsibility to see that her children receive an adequate diet, rich in minerals and vitamins which will lower their chance of contracting this disease.

Sister Kenny had great results with her treatment, about 80% of those whom she treated recovering without crippling, when the treatment was begun immediately after the condition appeared. In the acute stage, the muscles are in a state of spasm and hot wet compresses made of towels wrung out of hot water, should be applied to the affected area and renewed every 2 hours or oftener, the patient meanwhile being placed on a hard bed with his feet projecting past the end of the bed and being pressed against some hard surface. Continue this treatment till pain and soreness has disappeared—usually in about 2 or 3 days. Then muscle training must begin, gently massaging and manipulating the affected muscles. The patient should be encouraged to "think" the moving of the muscles. Remember the mind directs the actions. Gradually, as movement comes back, the child should begin to train the muscles. Each muscle should be tested and only the weak ones exercised, otherwise they will not be balanced. When working on the muscles at first, move them in various directions, but only so far as the muscles would normally go of their own accord, the exercise periods lasting about half an hour two or three times each day. In respiratory cases, the child should be taught to breathe deeply until the gasping stops and he can breathe normally again.

The diet should consist of raw juices only—for the first few days, and afterwards of natural foods containing plenty of Vitamin C, good sources being the juice of cabbage or the citrus juices.

In cases where a child has contracted Polio a diet-conscious physician should be contacted immediately.

Adenoids and Tonsils

Not so many years ago it was thought a necessity to have a child's tonsils removed. Tonsil and adenoid removal became the fad, and with the "Eventually, why not now?" idea, children were rushed wholesale to the hospitals. According to a reliable report, in one of the best equipped hospitals in the country, out of one thousand tonsillectomies, only 7% showed active disease, 30% showed where Nature had healed a former diseased condition, and the rest of the tonsils were perfectly healthy.

Tonsils and adenoids are lymphatic glands. There are lymph streams in the body similar to blood streams, but lymph is colorless. If you scrape your skin deep enough—yet not so deep that blood will flow—you will see lymph (similar in appearance to water), form in little beads upon the abraded surface. Lymph carries digested food to all parts of the body and assists in the healing process. The lymph streams also gather up waste material and carry it along to be eliminated. If there is an increased amount of waste material to be disposed of, Nature increases the size of the lymphatic glands to take care of the extra amount of work to be done. Thus we have "enlarged tonsils and adenoids." Usually, to have these removed is not only useless—it is foolish. If one simply cleanses the system and stops the intake of food causing these waste toxins, the adenoids and tonsils will return to their normal condition automatically. One would not have a thumb cut off simply because it was sore and inflamed, and neither should the lymphatic glands be removed. Nature knew what she was doing when she made you. Every part has an important role to perform.

The increased waste poisons which cause the swelling and inflammation or disease of the tonsils and adenoids are caused by:

1. Eating foods which cause the formation of acid poisons. These foods are chiefly white flour and white sugar products in any form, particularly candy, cake, pastries, white bread, refined cereals.

2. Constipation.

The cure is simply the reversal of the cause—proper diet and proper elimination.

Faster results may be obtained if, for the first few days of the treatment, the sufferer will take nothing but fruit and vegetable juice. Sometimes this liquid diet will reduce the tonsils and adenoids to a normal condition in a matter of a few days. If it is impossible to go on a liquid diet, then, in addition to the liquids mentioned, eat oranges and grapefruit, nothing else. Later finely-grated carrots, cottage cheese, and, in fact all raw vegetables and fruits may be taken. Attractive salads may be combined so one does not realize that he is on a special diet. Do not use salad dressings, milk, cream, starch foods, ice cream, milk or malted milk drinks, sugars, candies, breads or starches of any kind, as they tend to further enlarge the glands.

A sponge bath should be taken daily. Plenty of fresh air and sunlight should be had, without fail. If sunshine is lacking Vitamin D capsules should be taken.

It is very important that the bowels be kept open, as no cure can be expected if the waste matter from the bowels is being retained in the system. So a natural laxative or an enema should be given daily, if in the least constipated, until such a time as the juice and natural diet rectify this condition.

Local treatment—If the throat is much inflamed, it may be relieved by the use of an ice-filled bag, or by means of a cloth wrung lightly out of cold water, with a dry woolen cloth or piece of plastic material placed on the outside to hold the moisture and to protect the clothing. If the condition is bad, stay in bed. Rest, fresh air and quiet are essential.

A good cleansing gargle of lemon juice and water taken several times daily is helpful.

Carrot and beet juice are excellent, or carrot juice alone, if the child objects to the beet juice. Beet juice is very pleasant added to tomato juice. This may be given freely.

Rheumatic Fever

Dr. Alvin F. Coburn of the Rheumatic Fever Research Institute, Northwestern University Medical School, Chicago, told the American Dietetic Association, "The problem of preventing the disease (Rheumatic Fever) by nutrition merits a high priority in our daily thoughts."

This illness is responsible for more heart disease than any other. Chorea, or St. Vitus Dance, is a symptom of this condition, although sometimes there seems to be no special symptom other than the child appears to be more listless and tired than he should be. There may be loss of weight, constipation, headaches, and nervousness. There may be such symptoms as "growing pains" though this does not always accompany rheumatic fever. No complaint of pains in the legs, neck or behind the knees should go without investigating. There are usually joint pains and heart trouble.

However, rather than wait for symptoms to appear, how much better to build up the health of the child so this condition does not develop. If the symptoms are present, the child should be put to bed immediately and kept there, for several weeks if necessary. He should be fed a diet which includes an abundance of natural foods, and fruit and vegetable juices, and kept quiet. The less exertion, the less strain there will be on the heart, and so the less complications will develop.

Rickets

This condition is caused chiefly by a lack of calcium and Vitamin D in the diet. It is this vitamin which enables the body to utilize calcium, and without it the bones are not properly formed—there may be beading or deformity of the ribs where the cartilage joins the rib bones, also the chest may be deformed into what is termed "pigeon breast" or "chicken breast." The head sometimes becomes enlarged or malformed and there is frequently a curvature of the spine, the knees may be knock-kneed or bowed and the pelvic bones may be deformed. This is especially to be deplored in the cases of girls, as the results will be shown too clearly when she later bears children.

Rickets may affect the organs and nerves as well as the bones, but is more readily detected by the resultant deformities. It usually begins with restlessness at night and perspiration, as well as a swelling of the ankles and wrists.

The diet should include an abundant supply of fresh raw fruits and vegetables, especially the vegetable juices, with lots of sunshine daily. If sunshine is not available, then sun lamps should be used, or Vitamin D capsules, as it is essential that Vitamin D is absorbed in some way. Eggs should be eaten each day and liver and kidney several times weekly. Any starch should be of the whole grain variety. Plenty of rest, quiet and daily walks out of doors should be taken to build up the entire health level. If constipation is present this should be corrected at once.

The following quotation is from the Yearbook of Agriculture:

"Many children, while they may not actually be anemic, are often listless, lacking in vitality, and have very poor appetites. There are definite signs that the body's reserve store of iron is low and is not being replenished because the available iron content of the diet is about equal to the amount needed for the formation of hemoglobin, with no surplus for storage. A sudden spurt of growth, such as may occur during the adolescent period, or an infectious disease, which progresses rapidly when the resistance is lowered, may so deplete the body of its reserve iron that anemia will result."

United States Office of Education: "About 15,000,000 (75%) of the school children of this country need attention today for physical defects which are practically, or completely remedial."

Scurvy

With this condition, there is usually swelling and pain in the joints, and for this reason it is often mistaken for rheumatism.

Scurvy is caused chiefly through a lack of Vitamin C in the diet. It is this vitamin which enables the cells of the body to cling together, and without it there may be bleeding anywhere, but is especially noticeable in the gums. In severe cases there may be paralysis as the nerves are affected. This used to be a very common ailment, but has become rather rare with the improved methods of transportation of fruits and vegetables. All citrus fruits and most raw vegetables are high in this vitamin, cabbage being an excellent as well as a very cheap source. It should, of course, be consumed raw in the form of salads or, better still, some of the raw juice taken each day.

Pyorrhea is a mild form of scurvy. For more information on this subject, read the chapter on "Teeth."

Pin Worms

The eggs of the pin or thread worms are taken into the system by means of water or food and hatch out in the body. However, they would not continue to breed there if they did not find a suitable place for doing so. A suitable place is one which is clogged with rotting, decaying fecal matter.

Most treatments for the eradication of worms aim only at getting rid of the eggs and parasites, but if this breeding place is not cleaned up, it will probably not be long before they reappear. In getting rid of flies or mosquitoes, the proper method is to clean up the breeding places of these insects, and the same applies to parasites in the body. The first thing to do, then, is to clean up the toxic condition of the bowels and the worms will automatically disappear.

It is best to put the child on an exclusive all-fruit diet to begin with, allowing only fresh, ripe, juicy fruits in addition to distilled water and carrot juice. This diet should last one week and be followed by a natural diet consisting of fruits, vegetables and their juices, milk, and whole grain products. No fatty foods, such as cream or butter or oils of any kind should be allowed; no meat or fish or any foods made from white sugar or white flour. Candy, especially, is to be excluded as this feeds the worms. Raw grated carrots, should be given first thing in the morning before breakfast. In fact breakfasts consisting solely of raw grated carrots and nothing else have often worked wonders in driving the worms from the body.

During the all-fruit diet or on fasts, the bowels should be cleansed each night with an enema consisting of warm water to which a pinch of tobacco or a teaspoonful of oil of turpentine has been added. As the worms lay their eggs outside the body at night, there is often intense itching in the region of the anus. The child, scratching these parts, and later eating without washing his hands and fingernails, re-infects himself with these eggs. It is therefore important that the utmost cleanliness be maintained.

Only rigid adherence to a proper diet and cleanliness of the body, both inside and out, will rid the body of parasites, and this cleanliness will also save the child a great deal of trouble later.

Feeding of Children

The customary diet of children: soft refined foods, cereals, and mashed potatoes, is responsible not only for children's diseases, but for much of the weakness and susceptibility to disease of the grown-up. Children do not need quantities of soft mushy cereals; they do not need pudding, sweets, and all the other rich, so called "building" foods. What they need are the mineral salts and vitamins found in fruits and vegetables.

The child should be given raw fruits and raw vegetables in abundance. If he is fed properly from birth, he will have a natural liking for these foods. But if he has been fed refined cereals, and artificial sweets, his taste may have to be re-educated in order to enjoy the flavor of natural foods.

Children need raw apples, carrots, turnips, and beets for their teeth and gums to work on. They need all the fresh raw fruits and vegetables such as lettuce, celery, radishes, onions, spinach, cabbage, etc., for the mineral salts and vitamin content—to build bone, blood and tissue. They need food that must be chewed. It is from the soft food of childhood that people get their beginning as gulpers.

Don't force your child to eat. If he would rather play than eat, by all means, let him play. Skipping a meal will be good for him. It is a very common custom to make children eat regularly, and to make them finish their meals whether they wish to eat or not, under the delusion that so much food means growth. Food in an unwilling stomach is poison. Nature makes known to the child when food is necessary. However, this does not mean that children should be fed whenever they ask for something to eat. If a child does not want to eat at meal time, he must wait until the next time for his meal. It is often because he eats between meals that the child is not hungry at meal time.

No program of proper rearing will succeed if children are permitted to nibble between meals. This should be made an unbroken rule in the household where good health is prized, not only for children but for adults as well. Ingrain in your children the habit of never touching food except when they sit down to the table for their meals, and you will have given them something more valuable than all the wealth in the world. Nibbling has ruined many lives.

There is one exception to this rule. If your children are hungry in the afternoon, give them fresh fruit and some carrot juice.

Every meal, except breakfast, should start with a raw vegetable salad, or some raw vegetable.

It is important that the child be taught the dangers of drinking soft drinks. Parents are sacrificing the health of their children before the God of Profit when they allow the pop-vending machine inside the school houses. We are going down as a nation unless we place a better guard on the welfare of the child.

Juices to be given: Equal parts of carrot and celery juice or carrot juice alone. Start with small amounts and gradually increase this amount as the child demands it.

CHAPTER 21

TOOTH DECAY

Dr. T. M. Sheehan of the Seattle Division of the American Academy of Applied Nutrition stated at the B. C. Dental Association convention, "Children can grow up without ever having tooth decay." He said they just have to stick to the right foods which are: milk, meat, sea-foods, cheese, eggs, vegetables, fruit and whole grains; and avoid sugar, brown sugar, syrups, candy, jelly, ice cream, soft drinks, chewing gum, white bread, white flour, packaged or ready-cooked cereals, pies, cakes, cookies, or doughnuts. In other words, he said, eliminate concentrated refined sugars, white refined flour and excess fats. They get all the sugar they need from fresh and dried fruits.

He suggested substituting for candy, ice cream, and soft drinks: hamburger with cheese, on whole wheat bread, fresh fruits, vegetable juices, tomatoes, carrots, dried fruits and nuts. He suggested a proper daily diet being: one quart of milk, one egg, two ounces of natural yellow cheese or four ounces of cottage cheese, six ounces of lean meat, poultry or sea food. At least once a week they should have kidney, liver, sea food or sweet breads. They should have one potato daily (cooked with the skins on), one green and one yellow vegetable daily, one raw salad, some hundred percent whole grain breads, two fresh fruits daily (one citrus), cod liver oil daily and bone marrow on toast or in scrambled eggs as often as possible.

175

This sounds like an excellent diet for even an adult to follow, except for the milk, which most adults would find too mucous-forming. Raw vegetable juices, which are richer in the essential minerals and vitamins than the pasteurized milk, could be substituted. Carrot juice is excellent, also cabbage juice, which is high in Vitamin C.

Good teeth, as well as good bones, depend chiefly upon the supply in the diet of calcium, fluorine, phosphorous, and Vitamin D, B, and C.

In Deaf Smith County in Texas, it was reported, dentists cannot make a living. The soil is very high in calcium and fluorine and so the plants grown on this soil are also high in these minerals. As a consequence, there is very little tooth decay and people moving into that district find that their affected teeth stop decaying and no more cavities develop.

Vitamin D is necessary because the body cannot utilize calcium unless this vitamin is present. Most people obtain far too little sunshine, and so it is imperative that they receive Vitamin D in the form of fish liver oils or sun lamps, where sunlight is not available.

Vitamin B complex and Vitamin C are also essential. A lack of the former may result in Vincent's Disease, more commonly known as Trench Mouth. A lack of the latter usually results in pyorrhea, the incidence of this clearly showing how widespread the lack of this vitamin appears in the diet. These vitamins are found in practically all the fresh fruits and vegetables, but they are easily affected by heat and very soluble in water and so are lost when the fruits and vegetables are cooked. Most people either will not or cannot, eat large quantities of the fresh raw vegetables and fruit, so they should take them in the form of RAW juices. Especially where trench mouth or pyorrhea have developed, the gums are very tender and inflamed, so it is impossible to eat the coarse, fibrous vegetables, and citrus fruit causes distress. In these cases, raw juices are a MUST. Carrot, celery, and the juice from green peppers are an excellent combination. Cabbage juice is also excellent, being high in Vitamins A, B, C and G. The cabbage selected should be firm and as green as possible.

Hungarians, who are noted for their good teeth, eat hard breads which exercise the gums, increasing the circulation of blood to feed the cells of the gums and teeth, and also eat an abundance of green peppers.

Children have a natural desire for raw fruits and vegetables. Usually the mother is to blame if this desire is lost. They coax the child to eat cooked vegetables when the child would far sooner have these foods in the raw state. If the child is allowed to follow his natural instincts and given an abundance of vegetable juice to drink, he is not so apt to consume candies and poisonous chemical drinks. A Cornell University professor and a Navy dentist conducted a very interesting experiment. They placed two human teeth in a glass of a cola drink and left them there for two days. In this period, the teeth had become soft and had begun to dissolve in the drink. And yet the parents of

American children have allowed the pop-vending machines to be placed inside the school houses!

Almost every child in the so-called "civilized" world develops dental decay long before he has obtained his second set of teeth. We can see what is happening to his teeth, but what about his bones? In many children the bones of the jaws are not properly formed, and the second teeth are either crowded or very much misplaced. Look at the jaw formation of a person who has lived all his life on a natural "uncivilized" diet, and you will see how the jaw bones should be formed—good strong teeth set in a well-arched, well-rounded jaw, with the upper and lower set of teeth meeting easily when the mouth is closed. When one realizes that the digestion of food depends to a large extent on the mastication of that food in the mouth, one feels a great pity at the thought of the start being given our young Americans. There is a child just outside of Mount Vernon, Washington, who had both upper and lower sets of artificial dentures when she was only seven years old.

Dr. Bunting, of the University of Michigan, performed a very eye-opening experiment. Taking a group of children, without any dental decay, from an orphanage, he had them given candy every day in addition to their regular diet. After six weeks most of them had some teeth which had begun to decay, but this decay stopped as soon as the candy was again eliminated from their diet.

The terrible dental condition of the children of America can be traced largely to:

1. A deficiency in the diet of the pregnant mother.

2. A deficiency in the child's diet.

3. The consumption of soft drinks, candies, syrups, white sugar products such as cakes, pies, pastries, etc., and refined, bleached white flour.

4. A lack of hard foods in the diet.

Straight lemon juice, especially the sucking of lemons, has proved to be harmful to the enamel of the teeth. It has been stated, however, that the addition of rhubarb juice to the lemon juice will stop the harmful reaction, but it is better to take lemon juice diluted.

The tops of turnips are very high in calcium and also Vitamins A, B, C, and G, as well as containing Vitamin E, and so is excellent for both children and adults. This is best juiced and combined with a milder drink such as carrot, or carrot and celery juice. This combination has practically all the necessary minerals and vitamins (with the exception of Vitamin D) to build good, strong, healthy teeth and bones.

Every person should feel it his special responsibility to do all he can to give the children of America a better start in life. What are YOU going to do about it?

CHAPTER 22

FRUIT AND VEGETABLE JUICES

The following is a short synopsis of the value of the most common of the fruits and vegetables:

APPLE JUICE:

This is a good cleanser of the digestive tract, being mildly laxative. This cleansing action frequently causes gas distress, and so is not advised before going to bed. It is useful in cases of catarrh, sluggish pancreas, as a cleanser of the gall bladder and liver, and for rheumatic fever. On account of its silicon content, it is recommended for hair, skin and fingernails.

APRICOT JUICE:

This is a rich source of Vitamin A, C and G, as well as most of the minerals. It is useful in cases of catarrh of the respiratory tract, anemia, indigestion, gall stones, constipation, and for the skin, hair and nails.

ALFALFA JUICE:

This is a rich source of Vitamins A and B but its greatest value lies probably in the fact that it is rich in iron—about one-half pound of alfalfa yielding the iron requirement for the day. The juice is made more palatable when mixed with carrot or carrot and celery juice. It also contains practically the whole range of minerals, and so is strongly recommended as a corrector of any condition from which the body is suffering. The tender green leafy stems only should be used for juicing.

BEET JUICE:

Beet juice is not stressed nearly enough as almost miraculous results have been reported in so many cases of anemia, low blood pressure, suppressed menstruation, heart trouble, poor circulation and low vitality. It is a good blood cleanser as well as builder, and so is used in cases of eczema and psoriasis. It is not recommended where diabetes is present. In juicing, a little of the top should be used.

CABBAGE JUICE:

Cabbage juice hit the limelight in connection with its amazing results in clearing up cases of stomach and duodenal ulcers. It contains Vitamin U, the anti-ulcer factor. It is not very palatable, but the flavor is improved by the addition of celery juice, or carrot and celery. It is an excellent source of Vitamin C, as well as A, B, and G; it also contains an abundance of practically all the minerals, making it valuable for almost any condition of ill health.

CARROT JUICE:

On account of its sweet, delicious flavor, this is the most popular drink of all the vegetable juices. But it has much more than mere flavor to recommend it, for it contains practically all the range of minerals and vitamins required by the body, being especially high in Vitamin A, the healing vitamin. This makes it of inestimable value in cases of catarrh, asthma, hay fever, catarrhal deafness, bronchial trouble, lung trouble, for the liver, gall bladder and kidneys, or for any place in the body that is lined or covered with mucous membrane. It has been used successfully in cases of ulcerated and cancerous conditions, gall stones and kidney stones, for improvement of eyes, for beautifying the hair, skin and, in fact, for making any part of the body healthier and for restoring pep and energy.

CELERY JUICE:

This juice is almost as great a favorite as carrot juice because of its favorable effect on the nerves and also for its power to dissolve calcium deposits in the system, such as occur in cases of arthritis, high blood pressure, hardening of the arteries, and stones. It has had great success where there has been inflammation of the nerves, such as rheumatism, neuritis, lumbago, sciatica. As it is highly alkaline, it is valuable for correcting inflammation of the urinary tract, although it is not as healing as the carrot juice.

CHARD JUICE:

This is a vegetable which is not used often enough. It is a rich source of calcium, potassium, sodium, phosphorous, chlorine, sulphur and iron, as well as being a good source of vitamins. It is a little higher than celery in all the minerals except sulphur, and can be used at any time in place of celery.

CLOVER JUICE:

This can be used in place of alfalfa, as its content is very much the same. It has been used in certain European countries for all cases of cancer and also to prevent this disease. The whole plant, including the blossoms, can be juiced.

COCOANUT JUICE:

Reams have been written about the cocoanut. In India the cocoanut plant has been used for food, drink, clothes and shelter and is one of the greatest blessings of the poor of that country. On account of its fat and carbohydrate content, as well as its simple protein, which is easily digested, it is excellent for underweight. It is also excellent for digestive troubles such as stomach or duodenal ulcers or colitis, being rich in Vitamins B and X, and being very soothing to drink. It is also used in cases of liver trouble and nervousness.

CUCUMBER JUICE:

Cucumber has long been known as a beauty aid, when applied to the skin. It is equally effective when taken internally. The juice can be applied to the face and neck morning and night after thoroughly cleansing the skin. When juicing, be sure to use the skin, as most of the value lies there. It is especially high in silicon and fluorine, which is essential to the health of the skin, hair, and fingernails. It is also rich in sodium and so has proved to be very valuable in dissolving calcium deposits in such cases as high blood pressure, hardening of the arteries, arthritis, gall stones, and kidney stones.

DANDELION JUICE:

This lowly, much despised "lawn pest" should be used by everyone, as it is an excellent, as well as a very cheap, source of Vitamins A, B, G, and also some C, besides containing almost the whole range of minerals, being especially high in calcium, iron, potassium, and sodium. It is an excellent blood builder and purifier, and cleanser of the liver, gall bladder and spleen. It increases the flow of bile and saliva and so is a valuable aid to digestion. It has also proved its worth in cases of diabetes, liver, and kidney troubles.

ENDIVE (ESCAROLE OR CHICORY) JUICE:

This is another plant which needs to be given more publicity. It is extremely high in Vitamin A, the healing vitamin, as well as having a certain amount of C and G. It is an excellent source of potassium, sodium, chlorine, and calcium. It is recommended in all cases where inflammation is present, as well as for calcium deposits, as in hardening of the arteries, arthritis and stones. It acts as a cleanser of the liver and gall bladder and, on account of its high Vitamin A content, it is strongly stressed for weak eyes.

GARLIC JUICE:

Although garlic will not make you a social favorite it is, nevertheless, very valuable. It has been known for centuries that garlic-eating races have a very low incidence of high blood pressure. It is excellent for catarrhal condition, is germical, (especially useful in infectious conditions of the throat or chest), and is known as a worm expellent. The chewing of parsley afterwards helps to cleanse the breath of the odor of garlic.

GRAPEFRUIT JUICE:

Grapefruit has a value similar to the other citrus fruits. The ground grapefruit (skin and all) has been found very beneficial when used on varicose veins.

GRAPES:

Grapes have become famous on account of publicity given to the "grape cure" for cancer. Although grapes are low in vitamins, they are great cleansers of the body. They are useful in cases of anemia, low blood pressure, sluggish liver, catarrhal conditions, overweight and skin trouble, but should not be used in cases of inflammation of the digestive tract, or diabetes.

KALE JUICE:

This is an excellent source of iron and Vitamin A, and should be used more abundantly. It has much the same properties as endive and can be used in place of the latter in any juice combination.

LEMON JUICE:

Lemon is an excellent source of Vitamin C, as well as B and G and also contains some A and P. It has long been a favorite in cases of colds and flu, but has proved its worth in catarrhal cases. It is also recommended in rheumatic conditions, for liver and gall bladder, pyorrhea, scurvy, dropsical conditions, and as a beauty aid. Vitamin P is obtained by grinding the skins, bringing them to a boil and soaking overnight, drinking the juice. This vitamin helps to prevent fragility of the blood vessels. Lemon juice should never be used when there is inflammation of the digestive tract. In concentrated amounts it has a harmful reaction on the enamel of the teeth, so should never be used without diluting it. It is a strong antiseptic and can be used on wounds where no other antiseptic is available.

LETTUCE JUICE:

The green leaves only should be used, as the bleached head lettuce has little value. Lettuce is good source of iron and is noted for its beneficial action on the nerves. It is also valuable in case of goiter and indigestion.

MELON JUICE:

Most melons have similar content, but cantaloupes in particular have a very beneficial reaction on the skin, assisting in the clearing up of eczema and other skin troubles. It is also recommended for kidney and bladder trouble and for indigestion.

OKRA JUICE:

This is very beneficial in cases of inflammation of the digestive tract, on account of its mucilaginous properties, so a small amount, when available, can be added to the juice combinations for this trouble.

ONION JUICE:

This contains much the same properties as garlic, but is not quite as strong. Onions sliced, covered with a little brown sugar and allowed to stay in the oven till covered with juice, has long been a favorite of our grandparents for colds. Onion juice, combined with honey and lemon juice, is also excellent. It can be made and kept in a cold place. Dilute with boiling water when required. Onion and milk has long been known for its help in cases of dropsical conditions.

ORANGE JUICE:

The orange is an excellent source of Vitamin C as well as containing a good supply of A, some B and G and is also a good source of calcium and phosphorous. Children and babies should have a daily supply in order to build good teeth and bones and to prevent scurvy, rickets, and polio.

PAPAYA JUICE:

This has been well known in the south as a digestive aid, as it contains Papain and Papayotin, which are digestive enzymes. It may be used in all cases of indigestion or ulceration of the digestive tract. It also assists in stimulating heart action.

PARSLEY JUICE:

Parsley is one of the richest sources of Vitamin A and also is rich in C, B, has some E, and is high in iron. It is best known as an aid to the optic nerves, but is also recommended for improving the functioning of the female organs, for anemia, liver and gall bladder troubles, and for improving the skin and mucous membranes. It should be used in limited quantities—about one half glassful, well diluted with other juices, being sufficient to take during one day.

PEPPER JUICE:

The green peppers are an excellent source of Vitamin A as well as being high in fluorine and silicon, thus being of great value in building the skin and mucous membranes. They should be used more extensively. In juicing, juice the seeds also in order to get the Vitamin E content.

PINEAPPLE JUICE:

Raw pineapple juice is one of the most delicious of the juices. It contains, like the papaya, a digestive enzyme which aids in the digestion of foods. It is also a good body cleanser.

POTATO JUICE:

The Irish potato is an excellent source of Vitamin C as well as B and A and most of the minerals. It should be juiced, skins and all, as most of the value lies next to the skin. It has been used, with great results, combined with carrot juice, in cases of tuberculosis. On account of its silicon content, it is useful in building good healthy skin and mucous membranes. This combination has also been used successfully in cases of colitis, and for gall stones.

RADISH JUICE:

This is an excellent source of iodine. It has also been noted for its effects in dissolving mucous, and so is used in catarrhal conditions. It has been advised that this juice not be used in cases of arthritis, rheumatic conditions, gall stones or kidney stones or any skin trouble such as eczema or psoriasis.

SPINACH JUICE:

Spinach is one of the richest sources of Vitamins A, E and G, as well as containing a good supply of iron. It is advised for the correction of glandular disturbances, goiter, overweight, anemia, weak eyes, and constipation.

TOMATO JUICE:

This is classed among the citrus fruits. It is very high in Vitamin C, a good source of Vitamin A, and has some B and G. It is a good source of iodine and so is recommended for thyroid and glandular troubles. It is used as a blood cleanser, for improving the skin, and also for liver and gall bladder trouble, pyorrhea and scurvy. It is not recommended in cases of cancer.

TURNIP LEAF JUICE:

This is rich in calcium, as well as being exceptionally high in Vitamins A, C, B, and G, together with some E. It also contains almost all the principal minerals. It should be used in combination with carrot juice, whenever it is available, as it is helpful in the correction of almost all the ills which occur in our body. It is especially good for growing children, building strong teeth and bones.

WATERCRESS JUICE:

This is just as rich as the turnip leaves in all the vitamins and is a little richer in Vitamin E, but it is usually more difficult to obtain. It is especially recommended in cases of thyroid or glandular disturbances, particularly for enlarged spleen and goiter. It is a valuable source of iron and calcium and, when available, should be used daily.

CALORIES PER PINT:

Beet Juice—220 calories; Carrot Juice—217; Celery Juice—89; Cucumber juice—84; Romaine Lettuce—94; Parsley Juice—283; Spinach Juice—115; Tomato Juice—112; Watercress Juice—109; Apple Juice—250; Cocoanut Juice—700; Grape Juice—462; Grapefruit Juice—200; Lemon Juice—210; Orange Juice—265; Pineapple Juice—207.

Evidence Illustrating Importance of Minerals in the Diet

In certain parts of the country, surveys have shown that soils are definitely deficient.

Minerals and Vitamins are very essential to the growth of healthy vegetables. If there is a lack of any minerals, the plant cannot be healthy. As plants form the chief source of minerals and vitamins in human nutrition, it can be readily understood that a person, depending upon the amount of food he can EAT, might very easily get an insufficient amount of these minerals in the diet.

By drinking quantities of the juice of raw vegetables which come from different sections of the country, we at least have a chance to balance body chemistry. Furthermore, by blending with these vegetables which are grown in the surface soil the juice of alfalfa, which reaches as much as 20 feet into the subsoil, and taps the elements found there, we have a juice combination which is exceptionally rich in minerals and vitamins.

For Complete Catalog
of Natural Health Literature
send $1.00 to

BENEDICT LUST PUBLICATIONS

The Original Health Book People

P.O. Box 404

New York, N.Y. 10156-0404